**Michelle** challenges professionals aore deeply, and practice more conscio als with ASD acquire and apply social In building on her seminal work in social thinking, Michelle argues effectively for an important and more thoughtful alternative to behaviorally-based social skill 'training' approaches, which are so limited in honoring the complexity of individuals with ASD."

**Barry M. Prizant**, *Ph.D., CCC-SLP*
*Director, Childhood Communication Services*
*Adjunct Professor, Center for the Study of Human Development, Brown University*

**A compelling tour** with a long overdue destination! With some of the most difficult questions surrounding the social challenges in ASD as a point of departure, Michelle charts an informed rationale for social learning strategies. Dispelling myths in-the-way of social understanding, she connects behavior to thought, mistakes to insight, and confusion to direction. This is a trip worth taking!

After reading this article, I reconsidered its title. Sadly, I have to admit that it often is politically incorrect to step back, think, and work to ensure that what we do makes sense in light of what we know. That being the case, Michelle is definitely a valuable charter member of a small, politically incorrect club of educators in the field of ASD. New perspectives are the forgotten half of change; this article organizes the thinking that creates exciting 'unexpected' opportunities for people with ASD."

**Carol Gray**
*Specialist of Persons with ASD, Author, and creator of Social Stories™*

# A

# Politically Incorrect Look

at

# Evidence-based Practices and Teaching Social Skills:

## A literature review and discussion

By
Michelle Garcia Winner

Social
ThinkinGⱼr

Think Social Publishing, Inc.

San Jose, California

*A Politically Incorrect Look at Evidence-based Practices
and Teaching Social Skills:
A literature review and discussion*

ISBN: 978-0-9792922-5-5

Library of Congress Control Number: 2008902627

Published by
Think Social Publishing, Inc.
3550 Steven's Creek Blvd, Suite 200
San Jose, CA 95117
Tel: (408) 557-8595
Fax: (408) 557-8594

Cover design and layout by Elizabeth A. Blacker
rowantreegraphics@comcast.net

This book is printed and bound in California by Medius Printing.

Michelle Garcia Winner offers workshops on a variety
of social thinking topics.

To order copies of this book, learn more about her workshops
or social thinking in general, visit the author's website:

www.socialthinking.com

# A
# Politically Incorrect Look
## at
## Evidence-based Practices
## and Teaching Social Skills:

### A literature review and discussion

## By
## Michelle Garcia Winner

# Contents

# Acknowledgements

**This project** started as a challenge, and I have never been one to shy away from an interesting challenge. While meeting with me in San Jose, Andrea Walker, the director of the Orange County S.U.C.S.E.S.S. Project (a county wide training program for educators of students on the autism spectrum), literally trapped me in a corner in my house and forced me into a discussion about the evidence based practice movement. There was a powerful movement underfoot, she told me, and it was time I got my head out of the sand and voiced a response to the movement, no matter how complicated the resulting argument may turn out to be. Thank you, Andrea, for that wake-up call.

Her timing was impeccable, or maybe it was fate that I had also just finished reading the book *Freakonomics* (Levitt and Dubner, 2006). The authors posed an interesting thesis: if we ask a different question we may get a whole different set of answers. The light bulb went off in my brain, and I realized that within the realm of education we don't ask enough questions. In relation to my own work and this new exploration into evidence based teaching, the relevance was startling: what if we asked the question, "What are social skills?" ***before*** we started to measure our success in teaching them?

In the world of academia, Dr. Patricia Prelock stands tall as one of my heroes. I am honored she is willing to take me under her wing and offer academic guidance. She was extremely helpful in streamlining my thinking process about this book and gently prodding me to make a more powerful statement. Her endless encouragement accomplished its goal.

My work is further empowered by the dedication of Veronica Zysk toward making my thoughts and ramblings sound more intelligent. The visual appeal of this book is thanks to Beth Blacker, my inspiring creative director.

But the true undercurrent of this project, the force that makes me do what I do, is my father, Max Rodriques Garcia, a holocaust survivor from Amsterdam, Holland and my mother, Priscilla Thwaits Garcia. These exceptional people always raised my siblings and me to use our brains, to think and question, to never accept what people lay in front of us as the way it should be.

Mom and Dad: I have taken that message to heart.

# FORWARD

## Patricia A. Prelock, Ph.D., CCC-SLP

Theory of mind and the range of perspective-taking required for meaningful social experiences requires a synergistic set of communication, social and behavioral skills that the literature reports is often lacking in the repertoire available to individuals with autism spectrum disorders (ASD) (Baron-Cohen, 1995; Baron-Cohen, Leslie, & Frith, 1985; Happe, 1994; Perner, Frith, Leslie, & Leekam, 1989; Prior, Dahlstrom, & Squires, 1990). Unfortunately, the role of perspective taking and theory of mind is seldom considered in the decision-making processes professionals use to develop educational programs for this population. In her text, *A Politically Incorrect Look at Evidence-based Practices and Teaching Social Skills*, however, Michelle Garcia Winner offers a unique perspective on the role of not only theory of mind and the range of perspective taking required in social situations, but also the power of executive function and the ability to plan, execute, mentally represent specific tasks/goals and appropriately problem solve.

Winner challenges her readers to reconsider how we 'think' about social skills, reminding us that being 'social' is a complex experience that requires more than just learning isolated social skills. This challenge includes a consideration that we enhance our understanding about the well-documented social impairment in autism (American Psychiatric Association, 2000; Lord, 1993; Volkmar, 1987; Volkmar & Klin, 1990) to consider what is behind and required for success as a 'social being.'

She suggests it may be less about learning individual social skills and more about social cognition and social learning. Winner also poses important questions about the use of traditional behavioral approaches to developing social skills and facilitating social interaction that certainly have an evidence-base but may be focused on the wrong goals. Targeting inappropriate behavior is not likely to promote, for example, the ability to think in social contexts— which is at the heart of what she believes is the core social challenge for individuals with ASD. She posits that traditional evidence-based behavioral strategies are not designed to foster the "underlying thoughts, beliefs and motives that might explain those behaviors." Winner also raises the concerns many of us share when making intervention decisions regarding the intent, structure, implementation and effectiveness of traditional behavioral, contemporary behavioral and social-pragmatic interventions. She highlights what clinicians and families know – one instructional method is not appropriate for children with ASD who represent a diversity of strengths and weaknesses.

Winner emphasizes that the relevant literature, her professional experience and the values individuals with ASD and their families identify for successful social experiences paint a complex picture. Teaching social skills is insufficient, as it requires an "integration of complex networks of interdependent thoughts and actions in a complex organizational structure." Coordinating what you know from your past experience with your current experience, and utilizing those experiences to understand the intentions and expectations of others requires something more. Winner reminds us that the ability to process social information and become self-aware, self-disciplined and empathetic often determines the effectiveness of our social-emotional skills.

Michelle Garcia Winner has captured several critical points as you consider your role as interventionists and more importantly, facilitators of social thinking in individuals with ASD, specifically those with more advanced linguistic and cognitive abilities. First, be sure to define what you mean by a meaningful social curriculum. Second, make sure you share a common vocabulary, which can be taught and understood by the individuals you are teaching and colleagues with whom you are working. She even shares a common vocabulary you can use. Third, consider ways you might define evidence of change unique to each individual with ASD as we continue to struggle with our operational definitions of the "social construct." Fourth, be sure not to lose sight of the importance of language, and learning social skills in real contexts. Finally, don't lose sight of the "whole child/adolescent/adult" when you are planning intervention.

Throughout her text, Winner provides provocative examples of social adaptations we make as social beings and the likely challenges for those with less sophisticated social thinking. She emphasizes the importance of teachers knowing and understanding the complex nature of social thinking and the impact of this construct on classroom culture and the social content interwoven throughout the curriculum. Fortunately, Winner does not leave the reader to start the social thinking and implementation process without a foundation for intervention. She presents her innovative ILAUGH MODEL of Social Cognition—a more synergistic approach to guiding the development of practical treatment methods for both social and academic improvement. This framework can be used by parents and professionals, and is founded on what we have learned in the research about ways children learn, think and socialize but with practical applications recognizing the challenges of children with ASD. Winner highlights the value of cognitive behavioral therapy in supporting the needs of children with ASD who have more advanced linguistic and cognitive abilities as it focuses on "talk therapy" and shifts the locus of control to the individual with autism.

Through her years of experience with individuals affected by autism, Michelle Garcia Winner presents two cognitive behavioral frameworks, *Four Steps of Perspective Taking & Four Steps of Communication,* in her text. These frameworks are designed to help students recognize the synergy involved in social thinking and the dynamic processes involved in making a social encounter meaningful and successful.

Recognizing that several disciplines have an expertise that can contribute to creating a social thinking program, Winner emphasizes the importance of our team attitude. Her emphasis on the importance of collaboration in making a difference for students reminds me of some early team training I had that suggested attitude is 10% about what happens to us and 90% about how we react to it. Maybe we need to think about how best to prepare our students with ASD to react to social situations. Winner suggests we initiate cognitive behavior therapy focusing on social thinking and collaborate as a team of professionals to develop social thinking instruction that is respectful of and responsive to the unique strengths and challenges characteristics of individuals with autism. She offers some powerful strategies to professionals who are working to ensure children become social thinkers, effective communicators, self-directed learners, and information processors. Further, Winner succeeds in making us think about how best to "study" the evidence for supporting social thinking— pointing out the challenges of relying solely on the available research.

# Abstract

The concept of teaching "social skills" misrepresents the dynamic and complex process that is at the heart of social skill production. Before we can act socially, we need to be able to think socially. However, in general the fields related to education and counseling of school-aged students have failed to study the complexity of teaching social learning. Instead, they have applied behavioral teachings in an attempt to tidy up "inappropriate behavior" without exploring whether, and to what extent, the behavior itself is caused by weak social thinking.

Students who are challenged in the area of social thinking and social skills – individuals diagnosed with autism, Asperger's Syndrome, PDD-NOS, Nonverbal Learning Disorders, and others – struggle daily within an education system that is, at present, ill-suited to meet their needs. Our current education of children (both disabled and not) is based on the assumption that all students enter school with basic social thinking abilities in place. And therein do we fail our students before they even arrive at our classrooms. We assume students understand people have thoughts that may differ from our own. We assume students know how to learn by watching others. We assume students understand that knowledge can be gleaned not just from verbal communication and textbook content, but the vast realm of nuance, innuendo, nonverbal communication and environment that are integral parts of our social world. Furthermore, we assume not only that this social know-how is in place, but that students have learned how to use basic social thinking to regulate their own behavior in a group.

Complicating matters is federal public educational policy (No Child Left Behind) which calls for schools to use evidence-based practices in teaching students, especially students with disabilities. The reality of today's world is that strategies abound for teaching social thinking and related social skills, and many are resulting in significant gains for our students. However, few – if any – meet the criteria for being "evidence-based." As an educational community, we have not yet defined what we mean by "social skills" or agreed on common curriculum when we refer to "teaching social skills", nor have we collectively agreed upon a host of other definitions that must first exist before "evidence-based" practices can become a reality.

This lack of common vocabulary and terminology about social skills does little to help our students become better social thinkers and prepare them for the real world experiences they encounter on a daily basis. We pat ourselves on the back when a student masters an isolated skill such as waiting in line appropriately, but fail to appreciate the bigger picture: teaching a student to apply social skills and related social problem solving across a range of diverse contexts. We have put the proverbial cart before the horse.

This article attempts to raise awareness of the many complex and interrelated issues that are at the core of teaching social skills by exploring 10 questions:

1. **What are social skills?**

2. **What are the origins of social development? Is there an age when our social development stops?**

3. When do we use social thinking and related social skills? How do we approach teaching it?

4. In what areas of social thinking do students with social cognitive challenges struggle?

5. What impact do weaknesses in social conceptual information have on learning the standards of education?

6. How can Cognitive Behavioral Therapy address teaching social thinking and related social skills?

7. Given the complexity of the social realm, is there a framework for teaching social thinking and related social skills?

8. Who is responsible for teaching social thinking and related social skills? Is the same teaching relevant for all persons on the autism spectrum?

9. How does social teaching fit into what we typically call "education"?

10. What are evidence-based practices? How do they apply to teaching social thinking and related social skills?

There are no easy, clearly defined answers to these questions. Each question will invariably raise other questions. But it is a starting place, a launching pad for discussions among educators, parents, school administrators and the state and national education professionals who create policy and standards.

While we wait for public policy to catch up with the ever-present and growing needs of our students, this article will open doors to new understanding for parents, teachers, service providers and administrators about effective ways to teach social thinking and related social skills. Our idea of what constitutes "evidence-based" practice within the realm of teaching social skills may shift and change as a result of this article. What remains constant, however, is our collective goal to equip our students with the knowledge and skills they need to become as independent as possible and contributing members of society and the world at large. In that, we are truly united.

## Chapter 1

# Introduction to Social Thinking and Social Skills

*People think that if something feels easy to do,
the mechanisms behind it must be simple.*
*—Cosmides*

Our understanding of the cognitive and learning challenges of persons with disabilities – especially those on the autism spectrum – has evolved immensely over the last 10-15 years. Today, it is generally accepted that formal social skills training is germane to any treatment program for this population, starting from early infancy and continuing into adulthood if necessary. Within this diverse population of people with social learning weaknesses, social impairment is a hallmark struggle, and their challenges are not just within the realm of social actions. Irresponsive of their intellectual capacities, weak social learning strikes to the very core of their social awareness – to their ability to think and reason on a social level.

As an educational community, relatively little has been done to explore the depth and complexity of social skills instruction to those not born with these abilities intuitively programmed. We make assumptions and recommendations on treatment from our own highly social frame of reference, and seldom stop and analyze the very different social processing mechanisms at work in the brains of these individuals. When our instructions fail and these children or adults stumble along with hit or miss social learning, we continue to attribute their failures to their disability. In reality, it is we who fail our students and children by our inability to step outside our own innate social functioning and consider a new paradigm of teaching. In essence, to teach social thinking and related social skills, we need to understand how social thinking develops in neurotypical individuals, strip off the resultant preconceived notions about social development to get at the core of social teaching, and then build from there. We too often let our assumptions guide our instruction and end up starting at a level too advanced for many individuals, or offer piecemeal instruction unaware of missing information that thwarts learning. Without the requisite foundation of social knowledge from which to build upon, our students bob along, adrift in a sea of social misunderstandings that have little to do with their innate capacity to learn.

## Generalizing Social Development

By exploring what other fields have learned about social development in people and society, we, as educators, can make more informed decisions and create a range of treatment programs that are effective for students with differing social knowledge.

The fields of sociology, linguistics and anthropology explore how we develop and utilize our social skills to function as a greater member of society (Allman, 1995a). Professionals in these disciplines have "repeatedly demonstrated the systematicity of various forms of communication across a host of language and cultures" (Simmons-Mackie & Damico, 2003). What this means is simple: while communication is complex, many systems of communication transcend culture. The knowledge gained by these disciplines provides us with a better lens to view our students within the culture of the school and home day. Furthermore, the emerging field of cognitive science is actively exploring how neurological development from the beginning of life is responsible for our social and language development (Gopnik, Meltzoff & Kuhl, 1999; Hirsh-Pasek, Golinkoff & Eyer, 2003a; Marshall & Fox, 2006).

The overall conclusion from researchers is that the study of social development in neurotypical populations is overwhelmingly complex, regardless of how "simple" or "intuitive" the application of these social systems is perceived to be on a daily basis. Cosmides (Allman, 1995b) states, "People think that if something feels easy to do, the mechanisms behind it must be simple. We think it is exactly the other way around: Things seem simple because evolution has crafted amazingly complicated mental machinery that is up to the task, and makes it seem easy."

A critical element of social development appears to be the emergence of a Theory of Mind (ToM) starting in infancy, evolving across our years of development and into adulthood (Marshall & Fox, 2006). ToM is defined as our ability to infer a full range of mental states, which in turn cause actions, beliefs, desires, intentions, imagination, emotions, etc. (Baron-Cohen, 2000). The emergence of ToM is viewed as the basis of social development (Sabbagh, 2006). Without ToM, social development falters or is halted altogether.

## The Complex Nature of Social Learning

Our social development encompasses far more than our ability to participate in conversations or other active pro-social relations. Social thinking and appropriate social actions help us navigate a world shared by other people – people with differing thoughts, motives, beliefs, desires, and perceptions. Our world is built on social structures, structures that are not always clearly defined and are often open to subjective interpretation. Further complicating matters, social knowledge is age and situation dependent. What is acceptable and appropriate social faculty at age three may be viewed as immature or inappropriate at age ten. For example, when teaching a preschooler to cross a street, we tell the child to first look to see if a car is coming and then wait until the car passes before stepping into the street. As a preschooler evolves into a fifth grader, the student's social awareness expands intuitively and he learns that when crossing a street the student *does not* have to wait until a coming car passes before the student can cross. Instead the fifth grader looks to see whether the driver of the approaching car sees the student and recognizes the possibility of a crossing attempt. If the student thinks the driver is considering the student's motive to cross, then the fifth grade student has no hesitation stepping out into the intersection and expecting the car to slow down accordingly.

> Our social development encompasses far more than our ability to participate in conversations or other active pro-social relations.

Seemingly simple social skills are, in reality, quite complex networks of interdependent thoughts and actions, supported by an equally complex organizational structure. Once again, this structure develops without effort or concrete teaching in the neurotypical child; it's a normal part of the child's social development. Not so for the child with social challenges, and without a structure that helps the child organize and make sense of social learning, the child drifts even further without this innate compass to guide his thoughts and actions. This social organizational structure is called Executive Function (EF) skills, and they help individuals cope with the changing demands of different situations (Russell, 1997). EF skills are "required to prepare for and execute complex behavior, including planning, inhibition, mental flexibility, and mental representation of tasks and goals" (Ozonoff & Griffith, 2000). They include "the cognitive processes that serve to monitor and control thought and action, such as self-regulation, planning, response inhibition and resistance to interference" (Eslinger, 1996). Executive functioning across contexts may be more appropriately termed "social executive functioning" and contributes to an individual's ability to process complex social information conveyed through ToM. Social information processing is a multilayered process "through which comprehension, pragmatic knowledge, ToM and EF intersect" (Twatchman-Cullen, 2000, pp. 225-249).

It is not enough for an individual to have social knowledge. The student or adult must be able to systematically coordinate prior social knowledge within the context of the current situation, reading both verbal and nonverbal cues from the environment and people within it – whether or not verbal conversation is taking place. For example, a child standing alone during recess must still employ social reasoning skills, even though there is no interaction with any other kids. Social rules that govern his behavior are at play in this – and every – setting. Likewise, an adult walking into a new job site for the first time is also expected to have a certain level of social knowledge based on prior work history that he can transfer to this new setting. And, it is expected that he can quickly compare his historical knowledge to the present situation and adapt the social rules that do – and don't – apply to the new setting.

This is Executive Functioning in real life terms, and while ToM facilitates EF skills, language development is also mutually beholden to the development of ToM. These two concepts work hand in hand, one synergistically encouraging the other towards higher levels of sophistication. As ToM, EF and language skills evolve, the individual becomes more adept at understanding the nuance of others' minds, while at the same time allowing individuals to code language using increasingly sophisticated linguistic devices (De Villiers, 2000). For example, a student entering college for the first time draws on his knowledge of past education to help him understand the new and somewhat different educational environment of the college campus. The college freshman on his first day of classes would know from previous experience that he would be getting homework in every class, so he would not ask the teacher "Do I have homework?", but instead "Where do you post the homework?" To ask the former question would sound ignorant, and cause the teacher to have a negative thought about the student. However, the latter question demonstrates a desire to succeed and forethought on the part of the student. To understand language in a social perspective, we need to understand the intentions and consider what we know about the previous experience of the communicative partners.

Social intelligence is but one of many types of intelligences that work collaboratively to help individuals cope and function in the world (Gardner, 1993; Levine, 2002). Howard Gardner developed the multiple intelligence model of learning, identifying seven distinct intelligences people use to interpret the world around them: language, logical mathematical analysis, spatial representation, musical thinking, the use of the body to solve problems or make things, an understanding of other individuals, and an understanding of ourselves. Gardner (1993, pg 29) recognized that all people can be seen as having developmental strengths and weaknesses based on how these intelligences play out:

> "While some individuals are 'at promise' in an intelligence, others are 'at risk'. In the absence of special aids, those at risk in an intelligence will be most likely to fail tasks involving that intelligence. Conversely, those at promise will be most likely to succeed. It may be that intensive intervention at an early age can bring a larger number of children to an 'at promise' level".

As Gardner points out, learning can occur through various different pathways. However, active learning that arises from using one's social intelligence is a major contributor towards our ability to co-exist effectively with others across a range of situations. In his thought-provoking book, *Emotional Intelligence* (1995), Daniel Goleman draws on behavioral and brain research to postulate that it is not IQ that matters most in achieving success in the world, but rather an interrelated set of emotional skills encompassing self-awareness, self-discipline and empathy – all skills part and parcel of social development. Yet, social skills need to be learned "on the job" through meaningful interaction with others (Hersh-Pasek, Golinkoff & Eyer, 2003a). And, herein is the Catch-22 of social development within individuals with ASD. They lack a full maturational development of social processing and responding relative to their other intellectual strengths. Without the skills, they miss the opportunities to practice and hone their abilities. Without the practice, their skills fail to develop.

In typical children, social cognitive processing evolves steadily, with little fanfare, through active social learning as a child grows and works through experience after experience. While all parents and pediatricians are quick to celebrate a child walking and talking, few realize the enormous party that should be thrown when a child has established joint attention by 12 months old – one of the most pivotal and world-expanding social skills a child will learn.

On the flip side, the educational approach towards teaching students with social learning challenges is often greatly oversimplified. As Gardner also points out, "Our educational system is heavily biased toward linguistic modes of instruction and assessment and, to a somewhat lesser degree, toward logical-quantitative modes as well." We are linear-thinking when it comes to education and usually adopt a one-method-for-everyone teaching style. Furthermore, educators and therapists erroneously assume social intelligence exists and develops in direct proportion to one's IQ. Why make the time to teach something that everyone learns intuitively? Even with those educators who recognize the need for formal social skills teaching, the emphasis is often towards the production of social skills in the absence of additional instruction on the social thinking that supports these skills. This is especially true for those "milder" students with autism and Asperger Syndrome who have near normal to above normal verbal IQs. We assume they "get it" socially because of their extensive vocabulary or ability to expound ad nauseam on a favorite subject. Research demonstrates students can learn to produce discrete social skills, but often in the absence of "generalization" of the learned skill into other environments (Gaylord-Ross, et al, 1984; Ihrig, et al, 1988). In 2007, this author theorized a significant part of the educational problem related to teaching students "social skills" in isolation from larger social knowledge is that many professionals assume the students have the prerequisite social knowledge from which the skills should have originated. For example, we teach students the steps involved in giving a compliment assuming students understand how to apply that skill with different people in different contexts, including the possibility that we can use this skill to get our own larger desires met.

While much has been written about social complexity from the standpoint of sociologists, linguists, cognitive psychologists and anthropologists, relatively little of this information has been integrated into efforts to teach the meta-cognitive dynamics of social understanding. Knowledge gained from these disciplines is helpful towards developing treatment models and related plans for persons with social learning challenges. However, we need to move beyond defining and discussing the complexity of social development and start creating workable and meaningful curriculum to teach social thinking and related social skills.

## History of Social Skills Teaching

Historically, the idea of teaching social skills arose from the recognition of persons with autism – a diagnostic condition characterized by impaired social development and social abilities. When Kanner first recognized autism in 1943, persons given this label displayed marked impairment not only in social growth but also in cognitive and language development. This triad of deficiencies led professionals to create early teaching programs that were strongly based on behavioral methods. Typical social-communication skills, such as eye-contact or making simple requests, were identified as missing by the educator or therapist and then taught through the application of behavioral reward systems. It was assumed that basic behavioral principles, such as shaping, repetition, and reinforcement, would result in the child acquiring the needed skills.

Therefore, it became common practice to use applied behavior analysis (ABA) to teach students not just appropriate behavior, but language/communication and social skills as well. ABA has proven to be successful in helping children with autism develop increased social competencies. This type of teaching program is now broadly used with toddler and preschool aged children, and is often referred to as "Early Intensive Behavioral Intervention." ABA is a set of principles that govern treatment programs, and professionals vary widely in their application and execution of these principles. ABA program models include the more regimented, structured format of discrete trial training (DTT), similar to those created by O. Ivar Lovaas in 1987, but also now include more naturalistic ABA teachings such as Pivotal Response Therapy (Koegle & Koegel, 1999) and Picture Exchange Communication System (Bondy & Frost, 2002). Because it has empirical research to support its efficacy, ABA is considered a sound teaching methodology to use with individuals with ASD. Clearly measured improvement has been witnessed in the majority of students with autism using these different techniques (Perry & Condillac, 2003). However, how and by what standards we define "improvement" must be taken into consideration. Behavior-based methods seek to change behavior and may not necessarily attend to the underlying thoughts, perceptions, motives and beliefs from which behavior arises. While ABA can improve behavior – a monumental step in improving the lives of children and adults with ASD – historically we have focused on the behavior action itself, rather than behavior change arising naturally from an internal shift in self-awareness and social perception on the part of the individual with autism.

As the number of children diagnosed on the autism spectrum continued to grow, and in recent years in alarming proportions, our efforts to better understand and define this unique community of individuals has too evolved. Our behavioral treatments have been re-examined and refined to become more child-focused and flexible enough to adapt to the heterogeneous learning styles of individuals with ASD. Also in evolution is the very diagnostic criteria that defines the disorder. According to the Diagnostic and Statistical Manual of Mental Disorders – Fourth Edition, published in 1994 by the America Psychiatric Association (and revised in 2000 as DSM-IV-TR), autism and its associated conditions all fall under the broad umbrella category called Pervasive Developmental Disorders. PDD includes five sub-classifications: Rett's Disorder, Childhood Disintegrative Disorder, Autistic Disorder, Asperger's Disorder and Pervasive Developmental Disorder – NOS (Not Otherwise Specified). Asperger Syndrome is the latest addition to this classification (1994) and is differentiated from autism by the absence of any clinical delay in language or cognitive development, or the development of age-appropriate self-help skills. This is in contrast to individuals who qualify for a diagnosis of autism. They have qualitative impairments in social interaction, language and communication, and display restricted repetitive and stereotyped patterns of behavior. Often, but not always, they are also cognitively impaired.

To acknowledge the panorama of social functioning within the broad classification of PDD, the research and treatment community began to refer to this group as having Autism Spectrum Disorders (ASD). Yet while the term "ASD" speaks to the diverse social, language and behavioral functioning spectrum, it also collapses what is a very heterogeneous population into one descriptive label, ASD. This has led many to a false assumption that there may be only one viable treatment for individuals diagnosed with some form of PDD. This author has experienced, on numerous occasions, special education directors or program administrators contacting her, posing the same question: "What is the evidence-based practice for students with ASD?", implying they believe one defined treatment program exists for their students, no matter what their individual combination of strengths and weaknesses. This is highly dangerous thinking if our goal is to meet the educational needs of this population.

## The Call for Evidence-based Practice

The increasing numbers of students with autism and Asperger Syndrome in our school systems resulted in widespread anxiety and pandemonium as teachers unfamiliar with the disorder and its manifestations were forced to learn "on the fly" how to work effectively with these students. Instruction manuals were nonexistent, and it wasn't until the late 1990s that published books on teaching students with ASD could be easily found. Some educators adapted and were able to modify their teaching methods and curriculum to present material in a way that made sense to their students. Others struggled, without proper training and administrative support, left alone to deal with students who didn't respond to traditional teaching methods and "the way we always do it" mentality. It was at best, a hit or miss way of teaching students. However, as time passed, workable strategies from in-the-trenches teachers and professionals made their way into curriculum guides, books, and workshops for educators. The Internet opened up a new avenue of sharing effective ideas, and both parents and educators began to realize these kids could far surpass our current assumptions of learning potential. Hope was resurrected within the autism

One size does not fit all; one method is not appropriate for all. Successful programs are those that appreciate the individual nature of each student.

community that these kids could be taught and go on to lead functional lives, with and without support. Students with ASD were graduating, some going on to college. Real-life success stories were unfolding in homes and schools across the nation.

Then in 2001 the education climate shifted with the passage of new federal legislation, the No Child Left Behind Act. NCLB called for more scientifically based research (SBR) to be paired with our educational teachings (NCLB, 2002). "Evidence-based practices" – education practices grounded in research – became the new buzz word in schools and boardrooms across the nation.

What a tight spot for teachers everywhere to be in! To date, the only method backed by research for teaching individuals with ASD was ABA. Many bright, curious, creative teachers had discovered ways of getting through to students with ASD, but their teaching strategies were not "evidence based." Also by then, various different methods of working with this population had been developed, many achieving remarkable successes equal to ABA. However, not all had been formally studied, or had double-blind, placebo controlled studies backing up their efficacy. And so began the dilemma of teachers everywhere: how to meet the requirement imposed on them by NCLB to use only evidence-based practices, when the only evidence-based practice for this population was ABA – and even there, some methods within ABA were not evidence based!

As the heterogeneous nature of individuals with ASD became more and more evident, so did the appreciation that one instruction method was not appropriate for all students with ASD. The principles of ABA may facilitate some level of learning for all spectrum students, but ABA does not adequately address the whole treatment program for students with

ASD or like disabilities who have higher cognitive and linguistic abilities (Perry & Condillac, 2003; Simpson, 2005; Prizant, Wetherby & Rydell, 2000). Teaching pragmatics – the social use of language – and associated verbal and nonverbal social communication skills through behavior analysis discounts the core synergistic conceptual problems associated with having a weak social cognition. Social skills cannot be isolated and taught apart from context, from the Executive Functioning skills that support them, nor from the social thinking strategies that preclude the action. Furthermore, many studies now confirm that those who function on the higher end of the autism spectrum often have co-morbid mental health challenges such as anxiety and depression (Abell & Hare, 2005; Bellini, 2004; Farrugia & Hudson, 2006; Hedley & Young, 2006; Stewart, et al, 2006), indicating social emotional support goes hand in hand with social pragmatic treatments. Addressing the complexity of each student's needs, based on his or her personal social cognitive and social emotional challenges, is a precursor to developing effective and appropriate treatment for this group of students. One size does not fit all; one method is not appropriate for all. Successful programs, from this author's clinical experience, are those that appreciate the individual nature of each student and pair treatment based on the student's unique combination of social, behavioral and emotional needs.

Simpson (2006) points out that the requirement of using scientifically based research, while well intended, is difficult – if not impossible – to apply, given the complex and varied make-up of individuals with ASD. Simpson urges more thought be given at the national level to how we define "evidence-based practice", and the criteria we use to prove a treatment technique is of sound practice. At the same time, Simpson also encourages the community of educational care providers to take a deeper look at establishing treatment programs for students with ASD, based on key features specific to this population that will help persons with ASD cope better with their learning challenges.

It is also important to note that even at present, definitions for evidence-based practice vary from field to field. The American Speech Language and Hearing Association (ASHA) defines evidence-based practices as those that consider client-family values in combination with treatment evidence provided by experienced clinicians (2005, pg 1).

In spite of the disagreement of what constitutes evidence-based practice, and the immaturity of our instruction programs in general for students with ASD, public school system administrators are aggressively pursuing "social skills programs that are evidence-based", failing to appreciate the very complex nature of their quest as it applies to students with a range of social learning challenges. Few have stopped to ask pressing and highly relevant questions such as:

> "What is meant by the term 'social skills program'?"
> "How can we relate this treatment need to evidence-based practices?"
> "Is it reasonable to assume there can be one social skills treatment program for all students diagnosed with social learning challenges?"
> "Is it even feasible to gather research evidence on social skills, which by definition, are highly subjective, fluid and changing from context to context?"

## Relevant Questions Rarely Asked

The underlying reason to pursue evidence-based measures is to clearly define, as much as is possible, sound, effective treatment and education programs for persons with ASD. If we are to respond to requests or government imposed regulations that require their use, it behooves those professionals upon which this responsibility lies to first fully consider the nature of ASD in general, and social skills, specifically, to answer pivotal questions upon which these treatments will be formulated. Not all life-relevant learning can be neatly parceled out into discreet units that can be uniformly defined, and then broken down sufficiently into teachable segments for this population. That, in and of itself, poses a huge challenge when teaching social thinking and related social skills to individuals with ASD. Is it even feasible to think that evidence-based practices can be developed for teaching social skills? Other, equally important questions merit discussion before any evidence-based treatment program can be created. Questions such as: what, specifically, needs to be treated in these students? What is involved in the treatment process? What outcome is expected from the treatment? What challenges may the student continue to have across the lifespan? To assume there will be no lingering problems for this population post-high school, that any evidence-based practice will be sufficient to remediate autism, is to assume we can cure people with ASD. At this juncture in our understanding of ASD, it remains a life-long disorder, with varying degrees of symptom amelioration that fluctuate from individual to individual. Even if we could "cure" people of their autism, the larger ethical question arises: should we? A very vocal and growing group of adults on the spectrum suggest that not all persons with ASD want that option.

Yet, we must begin someplace. Both parents and professionals seek best practices when it comes to helping individuals with ASD learn and achieve their highest functional capacity in the world. Our job, as the educators and clinicians who take on the responsibility of designing such programs, is to continually investigate and question existing assumptions

**Is it even feasible to think that evidence-based practices can be developed for teaching social skills?**

about persons with ASD and the manner in which we teach and treat them. If we seek evidence-based practices for teaching social skills and social thinking, our first step is to thoroughly define the issue, then use this information to formulate intervention strategies. In essence, we need to apply the principles of behavior analysis to our own actions, and "take data" on whether or not our teaching methods are achieving real success. If not, we may need to rethink our methods, adapt and try something new. Success will not be instantaneous, nor will it be likely that one program will emerge that across the board, is equally effective for individuals with ASD. The very nature of the disorder – with its broad spectrum of strengths and challenges – precludes this. It's time to abandon the quest for a singular program to treat individuals with ASD – especially within the realm of social skills, and start focusing on patterns of thinking and processing that point us to common ground within the spectrum. We may discover subsets among this population for which one type of program achieves more success than does another. No matter how we think about this job before us, evidence-based practice implies that constant review

*It's time to abandon the quest for a singular program to treat individuals with ASD — especially within the realm of social skills, and start focusing on patterns of thinking and processing that point us to common ground within the spectrum.*

and analysis will be necessary as these programs emerge, are tested and retested. Time is both our enemy and our friend.

The remainder of this article poses many of the seldom-asked, but vital questions underscoring the development of sound social skills teaching programs for individuals with ASD. They task us to explore and consider the depth and complexity of teaching "social skills" to those born with limited social insight. Answers to these questions come in the form of relevant information from both research and clinical practice, and will hopefully broaden our perspectives enough to spur more creative thought towards treatment. This author believes that a synergy is possible that integrates principles of applied behavior analysis into cognitive behavioral and mental health teachings. Perhaps this will emerge as the basis for evidence-based social skills programs for individuals with ASD, especially those with higher cognitive and linguistic skills. At minimum, these questions steer us onto a new road to teaching social skills and related social thinking.

## The Questions:

1. What are social skills?

2. What are the origins of social development? Is there an age when our social development stops?

3. When do we use social thinking and related social skills? How do we approach teaching it?

4. In what areas of social thinking do students with social cognitive challenges struggle?

5. What impact do weaknesses in social conceptual information have on learning the standards of education?

6. How can Cognitive Behavioral Therapy address teaching social thinking and related social skills?

7. Given the complexity of the social realm, is there a framework for teaching social thinking and related social skills?

8. Who is responsible for teaching social thinking and related social skills? Is the same teaching relevant for all persons on the autism spectrum?

9. How does social teaching fit into what we typically call "education"?

10. What are evidence-based practices? How do they apply to teaching social thinking and related social skills?

## Chapter 2

# What are Social Skills?

Talk to five different adults, and each will probably have a different definition of "social skills." Probe further, and each will probably have different ideas of what constitutes "good" and "bad" social skills. Take this exercise to a community of Latino or Hindu families, and the answers will again differ – substantially. How are we to develop educational programs dedicated to helping students with "poor social skills" when we, as parents and educators, lack agreement on basic definitions? Our actions demonstrate that we believe there exists "one" definition, one commonly accepted description of functioning. Social skills are anything but singular, by their very nature. Yet, we proceed as though we know what social skills are, without having first considered fully their depth and complexity.

Social skills assist us with social adaptation (Allman, 1995a). That may not be the type of standard definition we seek, but it does give us relevant clues about the nature of social skills. Appropriate use of social skills means one is able to adapt to an ever-changing landscape that takes into consideration the environment, the people in it, the thoughts, beliefs and needs of the individual and others who share the environment – whether or not they are in direct communication – as well as individual and collective history of knowledge and experience. Simple, huh? Anything but.

Poor social skills generally arise from two sources: 1) an inability to communicate effectively, to express oneself in verbal and nonverbal ways; and perhaps more importantly, 2) an inability to adapt effectively across different contexts. Some individuals are strong verbal communicators but lack the ability to know when, where, why and how to apply their interpersonal skills. They just don't "fit in" despite their obvious intelligence and verbal capabilities. In the middle of the spectrum are people who just don't "get" how to communicate with others, or what to do in different situations. Try as they may, their brain wiring prohibits this seemingly intuitive sense others have. They stumble along, making one social faux pas after another, clueless. At the other end of the spectrum are people with limited or no ability to express themselves verbally, with and without an awareness of and sensitivity to their surroundings. Many of these individuals "get" social skills but are unable to express themselves appropriately. However, the majority of those without language often also have highly impaired brain networks of perspective taking and social understanding.

In real life, these social skills impairments play out continually. For instance, to participate in a classroom with reasonable success requires more nonverbal know-how of generally accepted social dos and don'ts and contextual cues than it requires active verbal communication. In fact, this is true the majority of time we interact with our world. Most instances where we have to monitor and possibly modify our social presentation occur in the absence of direct social communication. When we step onto an elevator filled with strangers, people adapt their behavior by stepping to the side and silently staring at the elevator door or floor numbers. It's generally accepted as what we do when riding an elevator. Contrast this with the social contextual requirements of joining a large dinner party. In this setting, even though the room is filled with unfamiliar people, each participant is expected to actively engage socially. The uncommunicative wallflower is seen as socially odd, unable to fit it, probably never invited back again. Instances requiring social understanding and social adaptation exist by the thousands during any typical day. The individual who struggles is easily overwhelmed.

Effective adaptation to an environment shared by other people happens on the fly, off the cuff. As much as we may rehearse appropriate social skills, encounters with people are fluid exchanges, requiring flexibility in thought and action. No two encounters unfold exactly the same. In any given situation, we consider what we know about the context (formal or laid-back; boisterous or subdued?) and the people within that setting (strangers, acquaintances, family, long-time friends?) to gauge what we can say and do to gain entry into the group. Our ability to engage in this social algebraic equation is done at a fairly unconscious level, often in nanoseconds of time. To complicate things, social adaptation is not only about engaging. Sometimes the appropriate or preferred social response is NOT to directly interact or communicate. Lightening quick thoughts and sensory input give us the clues we need to make a decision to act or not act, speak or remain silent, engage or walk away.

Our social *thinking* is an integral part of our social adaptation; our social actions only go so far. Social success requires that the individual have a social sense that recognizes and assesses all the variables that make up a social encounter. Social thinking and related social skills are at the heart of making decisions on how to relate to our environment and the people in it. Social thinking is the master key that unlocks all the other social doors.

Pragmatics – the social use of language – and appropriate social interpretation of spoken messages is no less challenging. Brown and Yule (1983) explore in great detail the multifunctional nature of communication, even at the level of spoken language. There is not one specific language utterance that is interpreted exactly the same way by all.

Ultimately the application of "good social skills" is complex, an active, fluid process that goes far beyond adherence to a set of behavior rules related to a specific context. Social expectations evolve in nuance and sophistication with age. Appropriate social actions stem from an inner social understanding that takes into account the individual, the social partners (if any), the environment, the cultural norms of that context within a specific community, and each participant's knowledge, affiliation and impressions of the other persons in the environment.

To teach social skills, we as educators must interpret what we are teaching much more broadly than we have to date; there can be no one definition of "social skills" that will drive instruction. Educators must understand the complex nature of social behavior and teach within a framework that is highly contextually driven. Our curriculum must go far beyond simply helping students learn the overt and hidden rules of social conversations, or practice step-by-step social actions. A student who cannot adapt effectively to the nonverbal expectations of the classroom will have little social success in or outside the classroom setting. Peers interpret, respond to and remember each other's social behavior from the beginning of their play group experiences and certainly by the time they are school aged. We must start early, integrate social teaching throughout all parts of a child's life, and view this as continual, ongoing instruction in the arena of life. Social skills are, indeed, life skills.

## Chapter 3

# What are the Origins of Social Development?
# Is There an Age When Our Social Development Stops?

The 1990s were designated the Decade of the Brain by President Bush; its impact on research and understanding of the brain overflowed into the realm of social development. Advances in neuro-imaging coupled with an increasing interest in exploring the subtleties of the mind have resulted in more research attention to social thinking and social relatedness. In fact, this interest spawned a new field called social cognitive neuroscience (Adolps, 2003). We now know more than we ever have about the origins of social development.

Social development starts prior to birth through embryonic neurological formations. Social functioning emerges as babies actively pursue learning through their experiences. Multiple books are devoted to revealing the research detailing critical and intuitive social growth milestones (Bronson, M. 2000; Gopnik, A. et al, 1999; Marshall, P. & Fox, N., 2006; Hersh-Pasek et al, 2003a). In just 36 hours of life, babies can distinguish between facial expressions (Field, Cohen et al., 1983); by 7 months babies can match vocal expressions of emotion to facial expression (Walker, 1982). Pre-linguistic infants may also be able to understand that people's actions are motivated by internal mental states, an early developmental feature of Theory of Mind (Kuhlmeier, Wynn & Bloom, 2003).

By one year old, most infants are pointing to show what interests them or indicate what they desire. Language development begins in earnest around this time. Normally developing children talk about things of interest in their world as well as what they desire. As they learn to express themselves they also continue to explore what others are thinking and feeling. Meltzoff (1995) demonstrated that 18 month-old infants will follow though to complete an action they saw an adult intend to do, although the adult failed to complete it. Children start to use emotional words such as "mad, happy and scared" around 2 years old (Bloom, 1998).

Marshall and Fox (2006) define multiple components working together in early development towards social engagement. These include perceiving and identifying social stimuli, the processes involved in the experience of emotion, and developing shared affective experience such as joint attention.

Our social development never stops; there is no ceiling to what we can learn socially.

A range of social, emotional and behavior regulation skills emerge through infancy and early childhood leading to shared imaginative play and ultimately cooperative play. As children's minds move into more abstract thinking, their play shifts from concrete (a car is a car) to more abstract play (a car can be an airplane). As they continue to evolve in their social thinking they also incorporate other children into their play, first by sitting near them when they play (parallel play) and then by playing more directly with peers. By 4 years old, children are not only playing together but they are pretending together (Hirsh-Pasek, Golinkoff and Eyer, 2003b, pp 205-244).

A typically-developing child's mind becomes highly socially attuned towards group participation by the preschool years. These social thinking and related social skills are critical for a child to succeed in most future academic and social learning environments: kindergarten, elementary, junior and high school, not to mention the college campus or job site.

Language, social and emotional thought, as well as perception appear to work synergistically on the same social cognitive team, moving a child along in social development. As these abilities evolve over the early years, more abstract social communicative skills emerge, such as narrative language (Tager-Flusberg, 1999a). Narrative thinking and narrative language skills allow us to conceptualize and share ourselves and our personal stories with the world around us – fundamental skills in forming social, emotional, communicative and academic connections in life. Children quickly learn to modify their narrative language, based on the context of the environment. For example, they need to share far less descriptive detail when talking to a family member about the vacation they experienced together as compared to explaining the same event to a friend who had not been on the vacation. Determining the level of information, emotions and sequence of events one speaker needs to provide to the other depends heavily on the level of prior knowledge about each other the communicative partners share.

Students who have difficulty with narrative thinking, or conceptualizing and describing temporal or causal aspects of events, may be unable to use narration as a tool for the kinds of thinking and assignments routinely required in school (Miller, Gillam & Pena, 2001). Narrative language is critical for being able to produce coherent written expression. If one does not understand how to sequence written information to help the reader follow the writer's thoughts, then narrative problems will result. Good narrative language requires the writer to consider the reader and what the reader needs to know and organize content in a way that the reader can follow the thinking of the writer. Even though writing is often done in isolation, it is an act predicated on social thinking!

This complex evolution of social adaptation/social communication does not appear to yield with age. It contributes in large measure to what we call "maturation" and "wisdom". Our social development never stops; there is no ceiling to what we can learn socially. Therefore, it is ineffective and impractical to view social skills instruction as a stand-alone curriculum, or a singular set of rules independent of age, experience and setting. Social rules change as we age. Third grade marks a developmental shift in social functioning: from the black and white realm of "right" and "wrong" actions into social behavior based on nuance and sophistication. The set of social behaviors we accept as normal for dealing with a conflict as a four-year-old are not those we deem acceptable during teen years, or young adults.

We are all active learners of social information across our lifespan. Therefore successful treatment programs for persons with social cognitive learning challenges will be built on principles that grow with the child. These programs will be:

1. Dynamic: driven by the unique needs and challenges of the individual

2. Constantly adapting: to be both "age appropriate" and responsive to the social and cognitive problem-solving abilities of the person

3. Ongoing: our social responsibilities increase in complexity as we age. It is unreasonable to think that early social learning instruction will result in students with no need of services as they age into adolescents and young adulthood. It is true that our students can show remarkable progress across the years. But even typically-functioning children struggle socially. It is daunting – and unproductive – to think we can "catch a child up to normal social learning", given that the peer group is always pushing ahead with their intuitive social learning, always challenging and revising social expectations and social behavior. Our teaching needs to keep up with the changing, shifting perceptions, morals and cultures of our world.

## Chapter 4

# When Do We Use Social Thinking and Related Social Skills? How Do We Approach Teaching It?

Perhaps the more fitting question is "when *don't* we use social thinking and related social skills"? And, the answer is: never! We use our social skills any time we are in the presence of people, regardless of whether or not we intend to communicate with them. We understand we can't mow the lawn in the nude, that driving a car requires that certain rules of the road be followed, or that committing certain crimes is against the laws of our country. The rest of the time, when we're "alone", we use social thinking skills to understand characters in a book or movie or television program, in reflecting about past or present experiences, and making future plans that may or may not involve others. Unless we live as a hermit in a cave, totally removed from society, we are constantly using social thinking and social skills. It is naturally part of who we are as social beings. (Actually, that hermit would still be using social thinking skills. Think about it.)

The expectation that an individual will exhibit appropriate social skills when in the company of others begins as young as toddler-hood and is certainly active by the time a child goes to preschool. The reason many parents send their 3 or 4-year-olds to Pre-K, or attend Mommy and Me classes at 2, is so their children can practice and begin to acquire – through social interaction – the prerequisite skills to ease their way into Kindergarten. By then, we expect that the young child will be able to process and respond to social information when participating during circle time, lining up for a field trip, at meal time and during group play. We expect the child can appropriately share toys, understands turn taking, doesn't hit or bite others, will follow the teacher's directions. These social expectations widen and take on more complexity as children age. There is a monumental shift in social expectations as the elementary child moves into middle school, and then again, when the student moves into the more independent world of college and employment. Typical children's social development occurs almost by osmosis – through observation of others and contemplation of how what is observed applies to their own life (or doesn't). Complex social information processing – often occurring in the absence of social interaction – is the glue that ties together actions and environment and helps the child mature into a socially savvy adult. Without the connections that social thinking provide, children lack the ability to take the perspective of another or recognize that other people are information sources for their own learning. Generalization of learned actions is absent and the child is unable to apply social lessons from one setting to another.

This extends into academic, too. The appropriate use of social thinking is a prerequisite skill within academic subjects such as language arts, social studies and history. Reading literature requires students to grasp the social emotional concepts being explored by the characters; social studies and history require social thought related to a person's motives, intentions and personal experiences (Hoyt, 1999; Tovani, 2000).

Interestingly, students who are overly distracted during group participation activities may be labeled a "behavior problem", when in all likelihood, the students' self-distractions relate more to their inability to understand how to interpret and respond in the group. It's not a behavior issue; it's a social thinking issue that leads to an inappropriate behavior. Recognizing this chain of events and the origin of the problem is a critical aspect of successful intervention.

To date our focus has been predominately on the social *actions* of our children or students or adults. It's natural that we attend first to behavior, for it is the behavior that is most in our face and often, interfering with our lives or that of the child or student. What do we do, then, to teach social adaptation? We create programs that teach *skills*: how to wait in line, how to say "please" and "thank you", how to raise your hand in class rather than blurt out an answer. Historically, educators and clinicians have assessed the student's skills, decided which social skills are weak or absent from a student's repertoire, and then devised instruction (often using behavior-based techniques) to teach the child to act in a certain way. What's missing? Attention to the social thought process behind the action. We fail to identify the social knowledge underlying the social skill and then teach the necessary "social thinking" that will result in the production of the specific social skills.

Our current emphasis on social action versus social thought can be especially confusing for very "bright" students who nonetheless, suffer social thinking challenges. We incorrectly assume that students who perform well on intelligence and academic testing also have equally advanced social thinking skills. This is a truly dangerous assumption to make when teaching students with any type of learning impairment. We must probe deeper into also assessing their social thinking skills. For example, a second grade student with an IQ of 150 loved talking about chemistry. In fact, he loved it so much he continued to talk about his beloved topic even when his listener got up from his chair and walked away from the student! The student continued to stare at the chair and talk, apparently unaware of how to adapt his language in the absence of a social partner. He may have been academically gifted, but he was socially clueless at a level that many teachers might not even assume exists. We don't regularly encounter people in our lives who don't understand that when a conversation partner gets up and walks away, we stop talking. This student did not understand this very basic social concept. Imagine the nuances of social interaction he also missed!

Behaviorally-based social skills teaching programs have achieved success in helping children learn specific social skills. However, a common criticism of the behavioral-skill based teachings is that this methodology is generally weak in encouraging students to transfer the use of this skill beyond the specific context in which the skill is taught (Gaylord-Ross, Haring, Breen & Pitts-Conway, 1984; Ihrig & Wolchik, 1988).

They teach a skill in an artificial setting and wait until a certain level of skill mastery has been achieved before teaching the child to use the same skill in other, more true-to-life settings. For some children, this type of regimented, repeated practice may be needed, but for most students with any level of social impairment, a behavior-based method, even one that is built upon generalized skill practice, does not teach the student to relate the specific skill to underlying social knowledge. The student may leave the treatment room with a social skill but not as a "social thinker", able to apply his social thought process across all environments.

To further illustrate how an emphasis on teaching social actions over social thought can impede learning, Simmons-Mackie & Damico (2003) describe that "social skills, when dissected into parts lose their overall contribution towards creating social competence. Once the skills are taken out and treated as a skill, they are no longer working as part of a social framework." Looked at it in this light, teaching students to produce specific social behavioral outputs without the associated deeper teachings about social thought and social context, is unlikely to be the most effective approach in treatment.

Consider how we traditionally teach the social concept of eye-contact. We have one general set of instructions we use internationally to teach students to improve eye contact: we say, "Look at me." When the student looks we reinforce him with a food item or token, natural reinforcements, or both. We describe this process as "social skills teaching."

Stop for a minute and consider the fundamental role eye contact plays in social development. Eye-contact is part of normal social neurodevelopment by a baby's second month of life. Babies intuitively learn to orient to a parent's face, and learn that this adult can better the baby's world through this shared experience, first by satisfying the child's needs, and then as a few more months go by, by supplying valuable information about the world around him. *Am I safe with this stranger? Did I really hurt myself when I fell down?* Babies make eye contact to get answers to these questions as new situations arise in their life.

At about 12 months old, babies acquire joint attention, another social developmental milestone that enlarges their world even further. A sense of shared interests and shared opportunities is the by-product of joint attention. Students for whom eye contact is lacking are not just lacking the skill itself. More importantly, and more fundamental to social development, they lack the intuitive social cognitive connection to other people and their social emotional minds. They don't understand that by making eye contact, important information can be learned about the world. An array of research demonstrates that once eye-contact and joint attention is firmly established in the first year of life, a door is opened for increasingly abstract development of the social mind, allowing for more sophisticated use of body language (index finger point) as well as spoken language (Baron-Cohen, 1995; Baron-Cohen, Baldwin, & Crawson, 1997; Tager-Flusberg, 1999b). Not surprisingly, given the underlying importance of joint attention and eye-contact in allowing us to adapt and relate to the minds of others, 80-90% of students with developmental disabilities can be determined to have autism if they lack joint attention by 12 months old (Jones & Carr, 2004).

Behavior-based instruction may, indeed, increase eye contact in a student, but it may bring about no positive change in the child's understanding of why we make eye contact, or the benefits of doing so. Dennis is a 9-year-old boy with high-functioning autism, with normal intelligence. He was fully included in a mainstream classroom, but because of his challenges in conceptualizing classroom activities, actively attending and his very literal interpretations of instructions, Dennis had a full-time paraprofessional for support. Dennis' IEP contained the goal "using good eye-contact" and teachers had been working with him on it for many consecutive years. However, even after years of instruction, when asked to "look at me", Dennis lifted his chin towards the speaker, but his eyes looked towards the floor. After conducting a social communicative assessment, it was determined by this author that Dennis didn't realize that eyeballs indicated gaze direction. He didn't realize that by looking at people's eyes, he gathered information about what people might be seeing or thinking about.

Instead, when he was asked to guess what his mom was looking at, he made arbitrary guesses about anything in the environment. Clearly, teaching Dennis to simply "look at me" was ineffective; he did not know what he should be looking at, nor the personal or social value in doing so.

As an alternative way of addressing eye contact, Dennis was taught social thinking and the related social skill pertaining to the use of his eyes. First he was taught, using concrete drawings and images, that eye balls were like arrows – they point to something: "make a guess about what people are looking at based on the direction you see the eyes looking." Once he mastered this concept (about three months), he then was taught that people are thinking about what they are looking at. His parents and paraprofessional were taught to teach Dennis across the day to "think with his eyes": "What do you think your sister is thinking about based on what she is looking at?" "I'm looking at this sandwich on my plate – what do you think I'm thinking about it?" Over the course of the next two years Dennis slowly started to look at people's faces and at the direction of their eyes. When his more challenged twin brother, who also had autism, came to the clinic one day, I observed Dennis talking to him in the waiting room. His twin brother was looking away at which point Dennis took hold of his brother's face, turned it towards him and said "you have to think about me when I am talking to you!" Teaching Dennis to become a "social thinker" is a process that takes time. Teaching skills can seem a faster approach, but to what end? Dennis had to learn to recognize and consider social information before he could respond to it (i.e., show an improvement in the social skill of eye contact), but it appears to be time well spent since Dennis demonstrated he could take his social thinking into any environment rather than only practice it in the therapy room. And, he gained an understanding of why eye contact is important – a pivotal skill that would open his world to other social lessons and social connections.

It is also important to consider how delayed Dennis, at 9 years old, was in acquiring this social knowledge and related skill. His inability to understand eye-gaze and its associated social thought meant he was more than eight years delayed in social development. As parents and educators who craft IEP goals for children with autism disorders, it behooves us to ask this vital question: Is it realistic to expect a student to learn social thinking and related social skills that have not developed for eight years within the span of a year of IEP goal teaching? It is important that we teach students a deeper more thoughtful approach to acquiring social information and producing the associated social skills. But, we must also respect the complexity of the social information they have to learn cognitively, that typical students learn intuitively, and usually much earlier in life. Social development is an incremental process, with one skill building on previously learned skills. It isn't an arena where we can simply select skills, one from column A and one from column B, and teach them unrelated to the larger whole of social connections and social adaptation in general. Parents, educators and students can only be left with a sense of frustration and hopelessness if our expectation for students' learning far exceeds a realistic developmental learning framework.

**Chapter 5**

# In What Areas of Social Thinking Do Students With Social Cognitive Challenges Struggle?

**M**any top researchers in the field of social cognition have described key concepts that appear to be pivotal in the development of the social mind: central coherence theory, theory of mind, executive function, emotion regulation, and sensory integration. Several of these concepts have been identified as significantly contributing to the social, communicative, and self-regulation processing problems experienced in varying degrees by all persons on the autism spectrum and also in those with related social-cognition disabilities. Each of these concepts is summarized very briefly below.

**Central Coherence Theory** (Frith, 1989) explains a weakness in concept formation. Persons with challenges in building central coherence tend to focus more on the facts or details rather than the conceptual whole. Many students and adults with high-functioning autism or Asperger Syndrome have explained that they "never know" what a book or movie is about, but they enjoy the details in the story. A person with more classic autism may play with the wheels of a car for hours, yet never recognize the function of or the object with which he is playing, i.e., a toy car. Other students with high-functioning autism may check off steps in a sequence (get bread, jelly and peanut butter, open jars, spread jelly on one slice of bread...) as they accomplish them, yet fail to realize the overall purpose of doing the related sequential steps (to make a PBJ sandwich when you're hungry). Concept formation is the infrastructure supporting most aspects of our academic curriculum (reading comprehension, written expression, organizational skills). It also is the foundation of social relations and the ability to live independently as adults through adaptive life skills (cleaning an apartment, paying bills, shopping for food as part of meal planning, etc.).

**Joint Attention and Theory of Mind** (Baron-Cohen, Leslie & Frith, 1985; Tager-Flusberg, 2000, 124-149; Jones & Carr, 2004). As discussed previously, joint attention involves a child recognizing that people may share information about their environment with others, and by using a functional point, a partner may indicated something noteworthy of our attention. Theory of Mind (ToM) describes the ability to understand that people have different minds, and then use active mental processing to compare or contrast our own and others' thoughts and actions. Throughout our lives we engage in a nearly unending process of trying to determine the mental states of others: their emotions, desires, beliefs and intentions (Wellman, 1990). Recent research has begun to explore the very early emergence of ToM beginning in infancy (Sabbagh, 2006) and the prerequisite acquisition of joint attention that leads to the fuller development of ToM (Jones & Carr, 2004). Like central coherence, ToM operates most often in our daily functioning below the level of fully conscious thought or reasoning, whether we are actively engaged in social interaction, or thinking about a response to a past or future interaction.

**Executive function skills** (McEvoy, Rogers & Pennington, 1993) describe how we effectively multitask, plan, organize, and implement strategies to work towards a goal. There are multiple types of executive function skills

(Russell, 1997) and we use them in projects of a tangible, concrete nature (building block towers when we are very young, to building bridges as a profession) and in those endeavors that are intangible, involving social, creative, analytical or abstract mental processing. The ability to use cognitive organization to develop effective concrete or mental plans has been recognized as impaired in most persons with social cognitive deficits (Ozonoff & McMahon Griffith, 2000; Prizant &Wetherby, 2000; Prelock, 2006). Social interactions require active processing of multiple stimuli (sensory, emotional, motives). Individuals who see all the details yet cannot organize or relate them are easily overwhelmed and in response, will withdraw inward, retreat, or become highly anxious. While the term "executive function skills" has mostly been used to discuss poor organizational skills, it is really a comprehensive, wall-to-wall level of information processing abilities that are integral to just about any physical or mental action we take. In the realm of social thinking, it's the toolbox that allows us to effectively use split second, multisignal processing, planning and responding.

**Emotional processing/emotional regulation** (Prizant, Wetherby, et al, 2006a; Attwood, 2003) is the ability to recognize emotions within ourselves and others, and regulate our actions based on these perceived emotions. It is a social expectation that we relate to others based on how we feel and how we are making others feel. Like the other core concepts mentioned above, emotional regulation is fundamental to effective social communicative skill development (Bronson, 2000). Social cognitive processing and the actions we make in response to this processing cannot be considered outside of emotional regulation; social regulation is emotional regulation. Individuals with ASD experience many challenges in emotional regulation, beginning at a very basic level with challenges in recognizing their own emotions. Many bright individuals with ASD struggle to recognize, name and gauge the intensity of their feelings or those exhibited by others. Their feelings may seem black and white, on or off, hot or cold, with no middle degrees of intensity. These individuals are often unable to establish self-calming and self-regulation strategies without outside assistance.

**Sensory Integration** (Ayers 1979) is "the organization of sensation for use." We learn about our world through all our senses, not just through mental processing. Students with ASD often have difficulty integrating sensory information. Any one or a combination of senses may be distorted. These individuals may be hyper or hypo sensitive, and complicating matters is that their sensory systems may fluctuate day to day, even hour to hour. Sensory disintegration makes it difficult for the body and mind to process and respond efficiently, resulting in students feeling out of balance (Myles, Cook, et al, 2000; Attwood, 1998). Sensory integration challenges potentially limit the information a student can absorb and process effectively, negatively impacting the student's ability to learn and behaviorally or emotionally cope with the complex world around him.

The take-home message is clear: teaching social thinking and social skills requires that we take into consideration the whole child, rather than pick and choose social lessons and then assume they wi[...] generalize across widely differing conte[...]

Most professionals working directly with persons with ASD and related disabilities will agree: the weaknesses in the concepts described above are far easier to identify than they are to treat. Researchers continue to debate the similarities and differences among these concepts (Beaumont & Newcombe, 2006; Happe, 1994;). Logically, it is easy to see how all of these concepts clearly overlap and work synergistically within the same individual. How can one fully distinguish between the multiple skills that characterize Theory of Mind as being different from social executive function? Doesn't a Theory of Mind require students to form central social concepts (e.g., use central coherence)? Isn't emotion regulation related to sensory processing as well as an ability to consider another person's point of view? How does sensory regulation impact a person's ability to process the social cues required to develop ToM? Interestingly research suggests, however, that teaching students to use better strategies to self-calm, execute a plan and develop a central concept does not guarantee they will achieve further development in ToM. The take-home message is clear: teaching social thinking and social skills requires that we take into consideration the whole child, rather than pick and choose social lessons and then assume they will generalize across widely differing contexts. Our programs must address all these core concepts and integrate them into a program that recognizes the complex social information processing systems at work in individuals with social learning challenges, regardless of their diagnostic label. The question becomes: how do we do this?

As educators we look for teaching methods that can be replicated, that have a reasonable amount of structure to facilitate such replication, and that provide us with ways to assess whether or not a strategy is working and if not, make appropriate changes. Within the realm of teaching social thinking and related social skills, this can be challenging. The abstract and not-easily qualified nature of the core social concepts, coupled with their interdependent relationship renders most professionals speechless when it comes to creating any type of organized, shared curriculum. We want standardized, logical, methodical teaching methods for a skill set that functions in a decidedly out-of-the-box realm of processing.

Recognizing this lack of connection between what the research has taught us conceptually about students with ASD, and the predominantly behavioral-based treatment programs of the 1990s established for students with higher level autism spectrum disorders, this author created, in 2000, the ILAUGH Model of Social Cognition as a synergistic framework to help guide the development of practical treatment methodology for both social and academic improvement. The ILAUGH model explores a range of social learning issues and how these relate to academic learning. It addresses many of the concepts described previously, providing the foundation knowledge and know-how to develop related treatment strategy for school aged students and adults. Conceptually, The ILAUGH Model is used as a guide by parents and professionals. It helps them understand their student's deeper learning strengths and challenges. It is not a curriculum model in and of itself or a step-by-step teaching outline. Every child with social learning challenges is different. The ILAUGH model gives us the framework and the tools upon which we create programs tailored to each child or adult. It is the strategies born from understanding our students' challenges that will have the most impact on their education and their lives.

**I = Initiation of Communication** (Kranz & McClannahan, 1993)
Initiation of communication is the ability to use one's language skills to establish social relations and to seek assistance or information from others. Many students with ASD have significant problems initiating communication in stressful situations or when information is not easily

understood. Language retrieval is difficult in anything other than calm, secure situations. Even within the higher functioning population with ASD, the student's ability to talk about a favorite topic of interest can exist in sharp contrast to how that student communicates when needing help or when attempting to gain social entry into peer groups. Yet, these two skills – asking for help, and understanding how to join a group for functional or personal interaction – are paramount for any student's future social success.

## L= Listening With Eyes and Brain (Mundy & Crowson, 1997; Kunce and Mesibov, 1998; Jones & Carr, 2004)

Many persons with ASD and other social cognitive deficits have difficulty with auditory comprehension. From a social perspective, listening requires more than just taking in auditory information. It also requires the person to integrate information seen with what is heard, to understand the full meaning of the message being conveyed, or to make an educated guess about what is being said when one cannot clearly understand it. For example, classroom teachers expect students to "listen with their eyes" when they point to information that is part of the instruction. They also indicate to whom they are speaking in a class, not by calling the student's name but instead by looking at the student or moving closer. Students repeatedly relate to their peers through nonverbal cues, ranging from rolled eyes to signal boredom, to raised eyebrows to indicate questioning to gazing at a particular item to direct a peer's attention. Clearly to "listen with one's eyes" requires students to have mastered the concept of joint attention – a skill that seems to effortlessly develop by the time a child is 12-15 months old in neurotypical children, but may be missing from the social repertoire of the student with ASD. Instruction in this essential and fundamental function of social interaction begins with teaching students that eyes share social information; not all our students understand this concept, nor do they grasp that listening requires full attention to both verbal and nonverbal cues. It can then expand to teaching students to relate to each other's thoughts through play and other activities of social relatedness, followed by extending the student's realm to attending to and processing increasingly complex cues that help students "listen with their whole bodies."

## A = Abstract and Inferential Language/Communication (Minshew, Goldstein, Muenz & Payton, 1992)

Most of the language we use is not intended for literal interpretation. Our communication is peppered with idioms, metaphors, sarcasm and inferences. Our society bestows literary awards to writers who are most creative with our English language. Each generation of teens creates its own slang; kids who follow along are in; those who don't, are out. The abstract and inferential component of communication is huge and constantly in flux. It is a mistake to assume that our students with social thinking deficits understand our society's nonliteral use of language. In fact, most of them don't! Literal interpretation of language is a hallmark characteristic of individuals with ASD. Yet, as educators we either miss this impairment entirely – thinking our smart, bright students must understand our nuanced communication – or it is addressed in the briefest of ways, with instruction dedicated only to explaining idioms and metaphors as part of English class.

Accurate comprehension of a communicative message depends first on the basic recognition that two codes of language exist: literal and figurative. It also involves recognizing and interpreting both the verbal words and the nonverbal cues that accompany them. It requires an individual to place the communication within the context of the social and cultural environment within which it occurs. Furthermore, the listener must take into consideration any prior knowledge or history involved and the possible motives of the person initiating the message. Finally, emotional maturity and social development factor into how well a person interprets what is being said.

Active interpretation of the motives and intentions of others emerges in the first year of life, and expands in complexity thereafter. Children quickly learn that mom's tone of voice speaks volumes, and that attention to only words is missing a huge portion of her message. As children grow developmentally, they understand that message interpretation depends heavily on one's ability to "make a smart guess" based on past experiences, what they know (or don't know) about the current person and situation, and the communication clues available. Language users *assume* their communicative partners are trying to figure out their message. By third grade neurotypical students understand that we are to infer meaning rather than expect it to be coded literally.

Abstract and inferential language comprehension appears to be directly tied to a person's ability to quickly and flexibly discern the different thoughts, perceptions and motives of other people – in essence to "read the mind" of another from a social perspective. For example, a 17 year-old teenager with high-functioning autism was visiting this author at her house. When the author tried to strike up a conversation with the teenager by saying to him, "I hear you are in the school choir", the teen responded with, "No, I am in your house." This is not sarcasm, but literal language interpretation.

Students who fail to expeditiously interpret the abstract/inferential meaning of language also struggle with academic tasks, such as reading comprehension, especially when required to interpret a character's thoughts and actions based on the context of the story and what one understands about the character's history and motives. Without the benefit of real-world experience, these students are unable to imagine how characters might think, feel and act within the story.

## U = Understanding Perspective (Baron-Cohen & Jolliffe, 1997; Baron-Cohen, 2000)

To understand the differing perspectives of others requires that one's Theory of Mind work quickly and efficiently. Most neurotypical students acquire a solid foundation in ToM between the ages of 4-6 years old. The ability to take perspective is key to participation in any type of group (social or academic) as well as interpreting information that requires understanding of other people's minds, such as reading comprehension, history, social studies, etc. Weakness in perspective taking is a significant aspect of ASD and other social cognitive deficits. However, like all other concepts explored in the ILAUGH model, one's ability to take perspective is not a black or white matter. In all likelihood there is a vast range of perspective taking skills across the autism spectrum (Winner, 2004).

## G=Gestalt Processing/Getting The Big Picture (Shah & Frith, 1993; Fullerton, Stratton, Coyne & Gray, 1996)

Information is conveyed through concepts, not just facts. When involved in conversation, the participants intuitively determine the underlying concept being discussed. When reading, the purpose is to follow the overall meaning (concept) rather than just collect a series of facts. Conceptual processing is a key component to understanding social and academic information. Difficulty developing organizational strategies cannot be isolated from conceptual processing. Students with conceptual processing challenges often have difficulties with written expression, organizational skills, time management and being overly tangential in their social relations.

**H= Humor and Human Relatedness**   (Gutstein, 2001; Greenspan, & Wieder, 2003; Prizant, Wetherby, Rubin, Laurent & Rydell, 2006a) Most of our clients have a very good sense of humor, but they feel anxious since they miss many of the subtle cues that help them understand how to participate successfully with others. It is important for educators and parents to work compassionately and with humor to help minimize the anxiety these children are experiencing. At the same time, many of our clients use humor inappropriately; direct lessons about this topic are needed and relevant.

Human relatedness – the ability to bond emotionally with others – is at the heart of human social relationships and the fuller development of empathy and emotional regulation. Teaching students how to relate and respond to other people's emotions as well as their own, while also helping them feel the enjoyment that arises through mutual sharing is critical to the development of all other aspects of social development described above.

## Chapter 6

# What Impact Do Weaknesses in Social Conceptual Information Have On Learning the Standards of Education?

With the passage of the No Child Left Behind Act (2001) Congress strongly encouraged public schools to teach students according to their states' educational standards. This was a way schools could demonstrate academic proficiency. The underlying belief was that in teaching students to acquire the knowledge that supports the standards, public schools could ensure their students receive a good education. However, missing from this assumption of proficiency is the underlying social component that drives academic success.

When a conceptual learning model, such as the ILAUGH Model of Social Cognition, is used to explore social cognitive processing required in our academic teachings, we begin to recognize that these concepts are central in creating the infrastructure for the language arts educational standards taught to all students across the United States.

Listed below are selected examples of language arts educational standards on the California State Essential Standards list (Association of California

School Administrators, 2003). Italicized wording in each standard indicates the social knowledge students must possess and be able to use fluently to be successful in the subject.

| Subject | Grade of student expected to be proficient at the educational standard | Description of the educational standard |
|---|---|---|
| Reading | 1 | *Respond to who, what, when, where and how questions.* |
| Reading | 4 | *Make and confirm predictions about text by using prior knowledge and text ideas (illustrations, titles, topic sentences, important words, foreshadowing cues).* |
| Reading | 4 | *Use knowledge of situations, settings and character traits/ motivations to determine cause for character's actions.* |
| Writing | 6 | *Create a multiparagraph expository composition: engage reader with clear purpose, paint a visual image in the reader's mind, conclude with detailed summary linked to intro/purpose.* |
| Writing | 6, 7 and 8 | *Write persuasive compositions: clear purpose, supported, organized; anticipate the reader's concerns or arguments.* |
| Reading | 9 | *Analyze interactions between main and subordinate characters in text (conflicts, motivations, relationships, influences) and explain why these affect the plot.* |
| Oral Media Communication: Pragmatics | 8 | *Evaluate the credibility of the speaker.* (hidden agenda, are they biased?) |

Education professionals from the federal level down to the classroom aide assume 4-5 year old children come to school with a solid "social operating system."

Clearly, social thinking is embedded throughout the academic curriculum. Students lacking social cognitive processing skills will struggle with academic assignments grounded in the performance standards for their age group. It is also clear that teachers do not teach all information required by students to be successful in these standards. With many of the conceptual language arts standards, a teacher's role is one of facilitator, to help students gather and process their social knowledge rather than directly teach the social knowledge. For example, by fourth grade it is expected students can "define figurative language, and find examples of it in their literary works" (Association of California School Administrators, 2003, page 46). However the fourth grade teacher does not literally teach students what figurative language is; instead she gives a name to it and illustrates examples of what we call abstract language – social knowledge students have been learning intuitively for years. Neurotypically-developing students begin to play with multiple meaning words and phrases when in preschool and most find great joy in reading books like the popular series *Amelia Bedelia* by Peggy Parish. Children understand by kindergarten that Amelia gets into mishaps because she is misinterpreting her instructions. (How many adults have stopped to consider that Amelia may be a young woman with autism or Asperger Syndrome?) Social awareness is already developing, and by fourth grade, teachers are helping students put labels to the way their brain is, and has been, processing information. So, what is the teacher to do with the student with high-functioning autism in her class who, because of different brain wiring, has actually never noticed or considered that language has two codes, figurative and literal? Her standard lessons are clearly not relevant to this student because these lessons assume prior social knowledge. What happens? The child is referred to the special educator or worse; his inability to keep up with the work is attributed to disinterest or he's looked upon as unwilling to learn.

As a whole our educational system, the standards we teach by and the lessons we have used for decades presuppose that the purpose of classroom education is to lay academic knowledge on top of a fully-functional social brain. Education professionals from the federal level down to the classroom aide assume 4- to 5-year-old children come to school with a solid "social operating system." And, therein lies the crux of the problem in teaching children with ASD and other social thinking challenges. Even educators who realize this fundamental divide often fail to perceive the pervasiveness of this social deficit in many children.

We assume children know how to ask for help. We assume children have the skills to work as part of a large or small group in the classroom. We assume children are able to work independently. We assume children have the prerequisite skills to play on the playground with others. But these assumptions go even deeper: we assume children can attend, that they learn by watching others, that they can imitate, that they know how to initiate communication, that they understand their own and others' basic emotions, that they are motivated by social reinforcement. On an even more elemental level, we assume they understand that people have different minds, different thoughts, and different ideas. Many educators cannot fathom that a child could reach age 5 and not have *any* of these social skills; it's just too foreign a perspective for them to grasp. Yet, these students exist and they are growing in number every year.

Given these often extreme social learning challenges, students with social cognitive deficits enter school needing education on two overlapping fronts, the academic curriculum as well as the social curriculum (Attwood, 2007). We must, therefore, ask ourselves: Is it realistic to teach both academics and social thinking within one environment, the "mainstream classroom", when the majority of other students in the class are developmentally on track from a social perspective? An equally challenging question is this: are these other students as "on track" socially as we think they are, or are we overlooking needs that exist on a more widespread basis than we currently imagine?

### Chapter 7

# How Can Cognitive Behavioral Therapy Address Teaching Social Thinking and Related Social Skills?

C ognitive Behavior Therapy (CBT) is a form of psychotherapy that was first developed in the 1960s and continues to evolve in its application. In a nutshell, CBT is based on the idea that our *thoughts* cause our feelings and behaviors, not the people, situations, and events in our environment, and that by changing the way we think, we can improve our life. CBT is anchored by three fundamental concepts (Dobson and Dozois, 2001):

1. Cognitive activity affects behavior.
2. Cognitive activity may be monitored and altered.
3. Desired behavior change may be influenced through CBT.

Professionals and research are beginning to demonstrate that CBT can be promising in the treatment of persons who function high on the autism spectrum and those with related social processing disabilities (Attwood, 2003; Anderson & Morris, 2006; Beebe & Risi, 2003; Perry & Condillac, 2003; Sofronoff, Attwood & Hinton, 2005). CBT is often referred to as a form of "talk therapy" that focuses on the present, rather than delving into the past to understand the origins of behavior, as most forms of psychotherapy do. Marans, Rubin and Laurent (2005) discuss the role

CBT strategies, such as learning an "inner language" to help individuals cope with stressful events, can play for persons with Asperger Syndrome.

On a whole, cognitive interventions, as described by Simpson (2005), attempt to shift the locus of control from the therapists, educators and parents to the individual. Simpson explains that thought and other cognitive processes are generally assumed to mediate an individual's behavior and performance. Thus, changing these factors in a person is likely best accomplished by changing an individual's perceptions, self-understanding and beliefs.

Many educators, OTs, SLPs and other related service providers working with students with AS/HFA over the years have developed educational teaching strategies that, in retrospect, mirror the basic principles inherent in CBT clinical methodology. Examples of CBT-like treatment strategies developed by educators include Social Stories™ (Gray, 2002), Comic Strip Conversations (Gray, 1994), the Alert Program (Williams & Shellenberger, 1996), The Incredible 5 Point Scale (Buron & Curtis, 2003) and Social Behavior Mapping (Winner, 2002, 2007a and b). These professionals – all without formal training in CBT – have come to the common conclusion that their students needed to be taught more about how their brain works, what information needs to be thought about, and given strategies to regulate their own internal thoughts and external behaviors to function with increasing success in social environments. It has also become accepted that concepts of CBT can be incorporated into social skills groups to bring about positive change (Howlin & Yates, 1999, Winner, 2005).

Gray's Social Stories™ (2002) are a classic example of unknowingly applying CBT principles to help teach socially-challenged students to cope with specific stressors. Social Stories™ are simple narratives that help students more fully grasp specific social scenarios, the related expectations and perspectives of others and appropriate social behaviors to use. Social Stories™ are an efficient teaching tool, conceptualizing these ideas using three discrete types of statements:

1. Description (what is happening in the situation)
2. Perspectives (what others feel or think) and
3. Directives (what to do).

Numerous single subject designed research studies have demonstrated positive results using this technique to help individuals manage more effectively in specific contexts (Toplis & Hadwin, 2006; Reynhoutt & Carter, 2006).

Comic Strip Conversations, another technique developed by Gray in 1994, helps explain, through visual supports, how thoughts and behavior are interpreted by different people. The simple use of comic strip stick figures combined with cartooning thought and speaking bubbles allows students to concretely explore the chain reaction or social algebra at the heart of social interaction, understand the origin of social conflict stemming from differing perceptions and thoughts, and provide a visual model of appropriate social communication.

Two other therapy models, described in the books, *The Incredible 5 Point Scale* (Buron & Curtis, 2003) and *A Five is Against the Law!* (Buron, 2007), teach students to explore the different levels of their behavior using a simple 5 point scale. A "1" refers to the "best" type of behavior controls we use, a "5" refers to our worst behavior controls – being out of control. Students are taught to explore how the different levels of their emotions and behavior "look and feel" and what strategies can be employed to help them shift their behavior to a lower, calmer place on their own 5 point scale.

Social Behavior Mapping (Winner, 2002, 2007a and b) explores the idea that all behaviors in a context shared by other people can be interpreted as "social behaviors" and influence our own, and others' thoughts, feelings and actions. In shared environments how we act leads others to have emotional reactions, which lead to natural consequences. When the natural consequences are positive, the recipient feels good; however, the opposite is also true. When natural consequences are negative, the recipient feels bad. Creating a visual map of expected and unexpected social emotional behavior reactions helps students learn the impact we all have on each other within social situations.

Each of these programs, in their own way, supports the greater goal of CBT: to increase a client's awareness of the impact of their behavior on others as well as themselves (Attwood, 2003).

## Chapter 8

# Given the Complexity of the Social Realm, Is There a Framework for Teaching Social Thinking and Related Social Skills?

**W**hile many parents and professionals recognize the need for formal and informal social skill programs as part of a student's education, the specific purpose of these programs often remains unclear. In reality, we cannot "cure" through cognitive and behavioral treatments a neurologically based learning disability. Therefore, what do we hope to accomplish? Is it to help students gain knowledge and skills that lead to increasing improvements? Or, something more? Where do we begin?

There is likely nothing more difficult than trying to teach social thinking and related social skills to a student not born with the "social software" to encourage active social self-learning from infancy. That said, an increasing number of professionals believe it can be done, and their success in helping students with ASD and related social thinking challenges proves that so.

An effective treatment program needs to define not just the skills to be addressed but, more importantly, the social thinking concepts we want students to learn. In our daily life interactions, we have to think socially before we can behave socially in the eyes of others.

One of the more daunting problems associated with this realm of challenges is the absence of a common vocabulary to describe social weaknesses. While we have a way to define and prescribe treatment for more traditional learning disabilities such as reading decoding and math calculations, we do not have a vocabulary for discussing students who present as "socially odd" or "awkward." The social realm is highly subjective and cannot be separated out from the environmental and cultural issues affecting it. Plus, not everyone is comfortable (or trained in) talking about social problems. We neurotypical folk tend to get emotionally involved in such discussions; in turn our judgment is affected. Talking about someone's social behavior may embarrass us or we fear causing offense in others. It becomes easier to assign broad, impersonal judgments – "he's just eccentric" or "she's a loner" – than to roll up our sleeves and pick apart social dysfunction to arrive at some common, usable vocabulary.

It is no surprise, then, that it is even more difficult to develop effective treatment strategies based on these elusive, subjective descriptors. More

It is an underlying social expectation of being human that all people engage in perspective taking.

commonly, our students with social thinking impairments are lumped together under the umbrella description of "behavior problems." We then create a behavior plan for a student, assuming an intact social brain; the plan most likely fails because we fail to teach a student cognitively why his behavior is interpreted as problematic. Or, in those rare instances where educators recognize social thinking deficits, we still merely scratch the surface, using general descriptors that have some common meaning – to us – but not to them. For example, we tell a child he has to change his behavior because it is "rude" or "inappropriate." (How so? To whom? In what situation?) If understanding behavior was that simple, wouldn't our smart students with HFA/AS understand these concepts easily? *That's exactly what we think!* So we keep teaching the same way, expecting them to "get it" and attribute all sorts of negative qualities to these students when they don't learn. It is we who need to change, we who need to understand their very real, brain-based social thinking challenges. Many persons with Asperger Syndrome or similar social thinking disabilities cannot grasp the very idea that others perceive them to be rude (Attwood, 2007, pg 65). Or that others find what is to them, a natural way of information processing, to be not "normal." We go on teaching the same way, assume social understanding and then apply our own behavioral expectations based on the presumed conceptual knowledge. Then we wonder why they "fail to learn"?

To help mitigate this recurring spiral of behavior expectations based on social assumptions, this author (2002) began to undertake a social anthropological exploration of the evolution of social relatedness, resulting in the creation of social thinking concepts and vocabulary. Out of years of direct interaction with this population there arose two social, cognitive-behavioral frameworks: the Four Steps of Perspective Taking (Winner 2000), and the Four Steps of Communication (Winner, 2005).

These frameworks effectively help students understand the synergistic and multistepped processes supporting social thinking. Rather than being static instructional curriculum, the frameworks were designed in a way that is flexible and responsive to the individual and the environment. These frameworks can be used by both adult caregivers and educators with individuals of differing ages and differing developmental levels of social thinking. They provide a common vocabulary and set of concepts that can be used to explore social thinking and related social behavior.

**The Four Steps of Perspective Taking** explain that social behavior is based on social thought; it is only after we think about others around us – and what they may be thinking – that we adapt our behavior according to these thoughts. These four steps occur naturally in nanoseconds of time in neurotypicals, often without conscious thought. Furthermore, it is an underlying social expectation of being human that *all* people engage in perspective taking, any time they are with others, even if there is no direct interaction.

## The Four Steps of Perspective Taking

As soon as I share space with you:

1. I have a thought about you; you have a thought about me.
2. I try to determine why you are near me, what you may want from me (motive/intent). You wonder why I am near you, what I may want from you.
3. Given that I know you are having a thought about me, I wonder what you are thinking about me. You know I am having a thought about you and consider what I am thinking about you.
4. I monitor and possibly modify my behavior to keep you thinking about me the way I want you to think about me.

You monitor and possibly modify your behavior to keep me thinking about you the way you want me to think about you.

These steps emphasize that virtually all of our time spent in the presence of other people requires active perspective taking (Theory of Mind), and that students exist on a continuum of perspective-taking abilities. Every aspect of communication and sharing – inside and outside the classroom – comes back to these four steps, and taking into consideration not only our own thoughts, but the thoughts of other people in our environment. This becomes one of the first steps in teaching students with social thinking challenges: I think about you, you think about me, and we act in concert with these thoughts we hold.

**The Four Steps of Communication** help define the synergistic and dynamic process we call communication. When a student doesn't communicate well, we often teach him to use his language better. However, these four steps illustrate that a significant amount of our communication is dependent upon how we use our social mind, body and eyes.

## The Four Steps of Communication

1. Think about others. I think about my communication partner(s). I consider what I know about them and what they know about me.

2. Establish physical presence. That includes how close or far away our bodies should be (an arm's length of each other), how we orient our bodies (turn our shoulders, head, hips), and use gestures. Furthermore, while our language allows us to share specific information verbally, our bodies also are an information source. If our bodies are overly rigid or overly relaxed as we communicate with others, this can be interpreted

positively or negatively, depending on the context of the situation.

3. Use your eyes to think about others. We use our eyes, and notice how other people use their eyes, as part of communication. Our eyes help us think about others and send clear communicative signals about who we wish to communicate with and who we don't.

4. Use language to relate to others. People in communication with each other want their partner to be interested in them. If you approach another person and only talk about yourself, people do not think you are interested in them.

Take note of how much time we spend teaching students the 4th step of communication without giving great importance to the initial three steps. We assume they know them. Yet, consider this: a student can successfully hang out in a group of peers using the first three steps only, but a student cannot successfully hang out with others using only the 4th step and disregarding the other three. By teaching that communication is a much larger concept that just using appropriate language, we begin to ameliorate many other aspects of social functioning, too.

In the book, *Think Social!,* this author (2005) details many additional social thinking vocabulary concepts that can help educators and families talk more specifically about social thinking concepts and impart valuable social information. Topics include:

- describing behaviors as "expected/unexpected"
- helping students monitor if their "body is in the group", "their brain is in the group" and if they are "thinking with their eyes"
- social language components such as "adding thoughts", "supporting comments" and "asking questions"

- avoiding social conversation blunders such as the "whopping topic change".

A common social thinking vocabulary helps parents, counselors and educators understand the framework within which they can "crack open" some of the presumed social concepts and create concrete strategies to provide our students with more relevant and understandable information about these abstract communication concepts. By creating vocabulary to describe what is happening during a moment of social breakdown, adults are able to more explicitly describe the nature of the social problem. Some examples of social thinking vocabulary are described in Table 1.

Table 1

**Perspective Taking:** (Thinking about others and considering what they think about you) Helping them understand that others have thoughts, emotions, intentions, motives, belief systems, prior knowledge, experience and personality.

**Social Thinking:** Means the same as social intelligence. Our students have a learning disability in this area.

Being a **"Thinking of you"** (thinking about others) or

Being a **"Just Me"** (thinking about yourself and only what you want to do) person: These are terms to define the difference between what people expect from you when you are part of a group and what they don't expect you to do when you are part of that group.

**Thinking with your eyes:** Using your eyes to figure out what nonverbal messages others are sending.

**Flexible Thinking or Flexible Brain:** Using mental flexibility to interpret verbal and nonverbal information based on different points of view or different contexts. This is the opposite of having a **rigid brain,** where one follows a rule all the time or cannot interpret subtle different meanings in language or expression.

**Keeping your body and brain in the group:** Understanding that to participate effectively within a group, our bodies need to look interested and connected to the group and our brain needs to keep thinking about what the group is thinking. We also teach that people can see when your body or brain does not appear to be part of the group.

**Your body rolled out of the group:** A student's body is turned away from or physically removed from the group; others notice that the student is not working as part of the group.

**Your brain rolled out of the group:** A student's brain (and thoughts) are distracted from what the group is doing or talking about; other people in the group notice that he does not appear to be working as part of the group, even if his body is in the group!

**Blue thoughts (good), red thoughts (not so good/weird thoughts):** Refer to how our actions, words and even physical dress or hygiene create good thoughts and weird thoughts in other's brains (i.e., the impressions that we make). All people create good thoughts and weird thoughts across a day. People remember the thoughts they have about others; if the student primarily implants good thoughts in people's minds then that is how the student is remembered. If a person plants a majority of "weird thoughts" then that is what people mostly remember. Behaving really well after producing a lot of weird thought behaviors still leaves people remembering the weird thoughts.

**Whole Body Listening:** Idea that the whole body (eyes, ears, mouth, hands, feet, bottom and brain) needs to be focused on the group in order to listen and show you are listening.

**Following hidden rules:** Not all rules are clearly announced. Most rules in our world are rules people figure out through observation and experience. If you are not sure of the rules you can ask someone. For example, a hidden rule at school is that you are usually supposed to keep your shoes on in school, even if you take them off at home.

**Doing what is "expected":** Understanding that a range of hidden rules exist in every situation and people are responsible for figuring out what those rules are and then following them. By doing so we keep other people thinking good thoughts about us.

**Doing what is "unexpected":** Failing to follow the set of rules, hidden or stated, in the environment.

**Make a "smart guess":** taking information you already know or have been taught and making an educated guess with the information.

**A "wacky guess"** is making a guess when you have absolutely no information to help guide your thought processes. In school we rarely ask for (or expect) this type of guess unless students are playing a game.

**People Files:** Visual way to help kids with social thinking deficits understand that we all are continually learning information about others and filing it in an organized way in our brain; we recall this information later when we see that person again.

**Social Wondering** (wondering about others): A concept that helps students begin to explore the idea that we are supposed to have a social curiosity about others and that we can NEVER know everything there is to know about someone. Social Wondering means you have a thought about someone's experience or beliefs and then you ask a question to gather more information.

**Asking questions to people about these other people:** Demonstrating interest in others by asking them questions focused on their particular interests or thoughts, rather than just on the topic of discussion itself.

**"Baiting" or "Bridging questions":** Questions you ask people to try and get them to talk about what you want to talk about (e.g., "Did anyone go to Hawaii this summer?")

**Add a thought:** When talking to others, we consider how their experiences relate to our experiences. We then add our own thoughts to help connect our lives to their lives. This is one form of a comment. When we talk to others we use different types of questions and comments to sustain and expand social relations.

**Figuring out other people's plans:** Determining what people are planning to do next based on their physical actions. We can also start to figure out what people are planning to do by interpreting the subtle meaning in their language, which is a higher level skill.

**Social Fake:** To demonstrate interest in someone else's topic that you do not find inherently fascinating.

**Boring Moment:** A set of socially acceptable behaviors one uses when he is not interested in what the group is doing at that moment.

**Whopping Topic Change:** When a comment is made and the listener cannot determine the thread of information that connects this comment to what was previously said.

**Tiny problem vs. big (earthquake) problem:** Helping the student put personal problems in perspective; understanding that problems differ in severity and our reactions need to match accordingly.

**The rules change:** Teaching students that the rules they are taught across childhood change, so they must undo some of the lessons taught to them as they age. A few examples follow of appropriate rules for an 8 year old that change by the time the child is 15 years old.

**Apologizing** by just saying, "I am sorry"; by 15 years old you have to show you are sorry through your actions.

**Hugging your parents** when they pick you up for school; by 15 years old you should just acknowledge them by looking at them and saying "hi" in a quiet voice.

## Best-practice Teaching Guidelines

As more and more educators and professionals have stepped into this new, exciting movement to explain and teach students the complexity of social thinking and related social skills, a number of common best practice instructional guidelines have arisen. Effective social thinking treatment programs seem to share the following principles:

1. **Tailor teaching to the child.** Explore, test and probe to learn the child's individual strengths and weaknesses, then design the treatment based on the child's individual needs. This is in direct contrast to creating a program based on a child's diagnosis. Social thinking will vary greatly, even within the same diagnostic label. For example, a diagnosis of Asperger Syndrome does not automatically mean a child needs 20 hours of discrete trial therapy along with four hours of speech therapy a week. Good programs take an individual approach; beware of "prescription" programs based on a label.

2. **Provide multisensory learning opportunities.** Learning is a sensory experience facilitated through multiple input channels. Verbal communication is only one teaching modality, and may, in fact, be the weakest channel in many students on the autism spectrum.

3. **Teach without assumptions of prior social knowledge.** If we teach social skills by encouraging students to do what is "polite" or to "show respect" they likely do not intrinsically understand what these concepts mean or how others interpret them. Our lessons must make the implicit explicit. For example, we assume school-age children

understand what it means to be learning as part of a group. We don't usually think to stop and evaluate whether or not a child understands that and has functional social skills that will allow him to be successful in a group situation. But, children with social thinking deficits often come to school without these critical skills. For example, a third grade "bright" boy with Asperger Syndrome raised his hand, eager to answer the math problem the teacher posed. When the teacher called on another student sitting next to him, the boy with AS angrily hit the other student because he "stole my answer." Even though the boy with AS sits in the classroom, and is very bright academically, he does not understand some of the more basic group behavior skills and the social thinking from which they arise.

4. **Evaluate the child's level of social thinking and start as basic as is necessary.** It stands to reason that we will continue to make social assumptions until we have a clear picture of the student's level of social thinking, perspective taking and social

Chronological age is not an indication of a student's level of social thinking; nor is expressive verbal ability.

communication strategies. And, our evaluation should be based on some level of objective analysis, rather than our own (socially-oriented) perceptions of what the student does, and does not, understand. In many cases, we may need to "move backwards" in a student's education once we have identified core social thinking skills absent. Take note: Chronological age is not an indication of a student's level of social thinking; nor is expressive verbal ability. We must evaluate to what extent our students possess pivotal social thinking strategies and start wherever we need to start. Given the difficulty creating standardized tests to measure socially complex, synergistic tasks, informal dynamic assessment tasks can be helpful in defining core social thinking deficits (Prizant, Wetherby, Rubin, Laurent & Rydell, 2005b; Winner, 2007).

5. **Teach flexible thinking as part of social thinking.** We can never expect our students to grasp and become proficient with the changing landscape of social communication and social thinking if we teach within a structured, regimented, unchanging format. The program must be able to adapt quickly to the needs of the student, in each situation, in real time, rather than making the student adapt to artificially contrived, teacher-led and teacher controlled social lessons. This means teachers must become comfortable with "thinking on their feet", quickly adapting lessons and grabbing every opportunity that presents itself to teach and reinforce social thinking (they are everywhere!). "Perfection" is not our goal in teaching social thinking and related social skills. Steady progress forward on a continuum of social learning is a more realistic way to approach it. The truth is that social learning never stops. For anyone.

6. **The treatment must be team oriented, with all teachers and parents "on board."** Our social world is confusing enough without the adults responsible for teaching the child making it even worse through inconsistent teaching methods. Social thinking instruction requires a multidisciplinary, if not an interdisciplinary, team. The team must establish a consistent philosophy which all participants adhere to and use to problem solve in the moment and teach consistent lessons across different people and settings. This includes home, school and in the community. A number of treatment models have recently been published that encourage integrated, school-based teaching that can be tailored around a student's needs. The most comprehensive educational approach is the SCERTS® model, developed over the last two decades through the ongoing work of Prizant, Wetherby, Rubin, Laurent & Rydell. The SCERTS® model is a synthesis of developmental, relationship-based and skill-based approaches that provides a framework to bring about progress in three areas: **S**ocial **C**ommunication, **E**motional **R**egulation, and **T**ransactional **S**upport. In 2006, the SCERTS team released a two-volume manual that guides parents and educators in consistently and effectively implementing the model. Other treatment frameworks, although more simplistic in nature, serve the same goal: to encourage teams to work together to facilitate teaching common social goals. These include The Comprehensive Autism Planning System or CAPS (Henry & Myles, 2007) and The Ziggurat Model (Aspy & Grossman, 2007).

7. **Hold all people accountable, including the student.** An important aspect of any social thinking treatment program

is holding people accountable to the program. This, in and of itself, is an important social skill, one that should be actively reinforced in the student and the adults governing the program. What good is it to spend time creating individual programs if we do not make the student responsible for using them? Parents, counselors and educators equally share this responsibility and are accountable to each other, and the student, to do their best to understand the presenting social challenges from a deeper perspective and analyze which lessons need to be explored, reinforced and/or modified to assure the student learns.

8. **The program should be meaningful to the student.** Not all students with social learning challenges feel the intrinsic need to connect with the rest of the world. In addition to teaching "how", we need to help these students find meaning in the "why" of social connections. We must explore their social interests and without judgment, devise ways to motivate these students, i.e., help them find "what's in it for them." Social learning is difficult and often laborious, requiring sometimes years of patient involvement. Students must understand how this knowledge will benefit them and can be applied across a range of situations in their daily lives. Otherwise they may think, why try?

9. **Include peers who share space with the students for whom the treatment program is designed.** To a greater or lesser extent, we can all benefit from social instruction. Demystify the social challenges these students face by extending instruction to all students on campus. In this way, everyone

*We must devise ways to motivate these students, i.e., help them find "what's in it for them."*

develops a greater appreciation for the fact that social learning is *NOT* intuitive to all and that each of us sits on a different spot in the vast spectrum of social abilities.

10. **Go beyond teaching "friendship skills."** Quality social thinking programs recognize and teach that life involves learning to effectively navigate positive and negative social experiences. Learning to relate to people you do not like as well as people you do like is at the heart of problem solving and negotiation skills. In the past this author described and provided instructions for students to keep "friendship files" in their brains to remember information about their friends. In reality we should teach students we keep "people files" in our brain to remind ourselves of information about whomever we encounter on a regular basis.

11. **Teach a definition of "social."** Being social is a nebulous concept for most of our students. They just don't understand what that means on a global level. Or, students equate it as all

about fun. It is important that we make it more concrete by defining "social" in a way that generalizes across situations in the student's life. The definition this author uses in her treatment program is this: *"Social" is being able to adapt effectively across different contexts and people.* It's equally important to stress that being social is a *skill*, one that involves learning, motivation and dedication. We teach students by middle school that social expertise involves "work"; we work at being friendly or cooperative even when we don't feel like it at times!

12. **Just do it!** At times the mere thought of the many different and subjective aspects of social thinking and social education can overwhelm an educator and inertia can easily set it. Start slowly and build. Realize that this is a learning process for you as well as the student. Until you both become more proficient, you will make mistakes and the early learning stages may feel uncomfortable. Just don't give up! The progress you see in the student will reinforce you to incorporate more and more social instruction into your daily teaching. Use the social tools, social thinking vocabulary and related instruction frameworks to teach yourself, your students and their caregivers to speak more specifically about social concepts. Being able to define the problem is the first step to solving it.

While the field of instruction in social thinking and related social skills is yet in its infancy, many clinical professionals are jumping on board to address the needs of this growing population. With their creative thought and professional backgrounds, especially in the understanding of the different thinking patterns of individuals with ASD, we are slowly expanding treatment methodology to help students learn more about social relationships, social understanding, social regulation and appropriate social skills. The real gain in our understanding has been in moving beyond the idea of teaching individual social skills, to generalizing this understanding so students learn skills that can be adapted across contexts, not for just a 12 week semester or school year, but over the long term, gaining knowledge they can use into adulthood.

### Chapter 9

# Who is Responsible for Teaching Social Thinking and Related Social Skills?

# Is the Same Teaching Relevant for All Persons on the Autism Spectrum?

The quick answer to the first question, of course, is *everyone*! On a more practical level, it is impossible to identify one professional care provider as the sole teacher of social thinking and related social skills to students not intuitively born to social knowledge. To date, no single profession devotes even a part of its program to social thinking. Until that situation changes (and we hope that is soon!) learning opportunities must arise from a range of professionals, ideally through the coordinated efforts of the interdisciplinary team mentioned previously.

Speech language pathologists are taught to be aware of social pragmatics and the "use" of communication to accomplish social goals, but few graduate school programs delve into the complexity of this area, teach professionals to become proficient in the realm of social thinking, and then translate this awareness into comprehensive clinical treatment approaches. Psychologists and mental health counselors are skilled at exploring the social emotional complexities of the mind for persons with reasonable perspective taking skills, but their teaching programs generally fail to consider how to teach social emotional information to persons who cannot take or understand another's perspective. Occupational therapists can help prepare the body and mind for learning but are not taught specific strategies related to the social executive functioning challenges of this population. Teachers and behaviorists are effective at teaching students specific skills, but have difficulties defining the broader social lessons in ways that are meaningful to students with social thinking deficits. Parents responsible for teaching social skills to their children in their homes and communities are not prepared for the challenges of children who do not actively and intuitively learn social thinking and related skills in their early years of life as a by-product of coexisting with others.

While it is true that a wider range of professionals are expressing far more interest in autism spectrum disorders than at any time in our history, "autism" is still a nebulous black hole for many professionals. A disability that robs individuals of ways of thinking and acting that seem innate to human beings in general naturally causes a certain amount of unrest and stress in people who see themselves as "the experts" in guiding treatment.

Social cognitive teaching is best suited for those students who function at the higher end of the autism spectrum or those diagnosed with Asperger Syndrome.

Therefore, larger professional associations are not quickly adapting their curriculum to teach their graduate students this newer information about social thinking. In fact, when this author was asked to speak at grand rounds to a team of well-respected psychiatrists who worked for a large urban hospital, she was told "be nice, be careful with these folks; they are afraid of autism."

Nonetheless, there are handfuls of professionals across different domains who recognize the central, overriding role social thinking has in the learning and future success of individuals with ASD, and are making headway in this area of teaching and learning. In most cases, this information sifts down to speech language pathologists, in particular, and they tend to be viewed as the "lead" profession in school districts in tackling the area of social thinking and related social skills. Even so, their graduate school education lags behind in addressing the complexity of social emotional communicative competence as reviewed in this article. So, now what?

We work together and take it one student at a time. The input from each of the professions mentioned above contributes to a better understanding of the mental processes and learning styles of our students. Furthermore, the personal insight into a student offered by his or her parents is invaluable in establishing a strong treatment team. While a large team will not necessarily be working with each child on the autism spectrum, it is important for us to always consider ourselves interdisciplinary, and let professionals flow into and out of the team as needed.

As important as the range of professionals who make up the team, is the team "attitude" itself. Any attempt to discuss and define social thinking requires group members who respect the range of challenges these students present; who can, without judgment, put aside preconceived notions of social competence; and are willing – and comfortable – with thinking "outside the box" of their professional training. Not everyone can do this. Consequently, the best person to take the lead role on a team is the person who is most curious and actively interested in learning about the student, embarking on an unbiased exploration into his social strengths and weaknesses, and is motivated and organized enough to then coordinate lessons across the professions. At times this person is the speech language pathologist or school psychologist, but it can also be the behaviorist, special education teacher, etc. This author has even worked with paraprofessionals who have become the "social thinking specialist" in the district for students with ASD. Parents are concerned with helping their children now, with finding people who are willing to take charge and find a way to give these students the social thinking skills that will make them successful in the future. There is precious little time to wait for clinical services to be developed while professional education systems slowly catch up to needs that exist today.

At the same time, professional fields of study must acknowledge and respond to this urgent call to action to begin teaching concepts related to social understanding, social thinking and related social skills. University programs must start addressing the varied and complex nature of social relations within their curriculums for all disciplines related to the diagnosis and treatment of autism spectrum disorders and persons with related disabilities (ADHD, Nonverbal Learning Disorders, etc). While this author was trained as a speech language pathologist, her years of work in the area of social thinking may be the harbinger of a new field, one of the "social cognitive specialist" – a professional who understands the inter-relatedness of challenges faced by people with ASD and has working knowledge in areas such as occupational therapy, speech/

language/communication, behavior, social skills/social thinking, academic education, and counseling.

Any discussion of who should teach social thinking and related social skills is incomplete without also considering to what extent this type of teaching is applicable to all students with social impairments. Fortunately, that answer is more concrete. Social cognitive teaching is best suited for those students who function at the higher end of the autism spectrum or those diagnosed with Asperger Syndrome. It is generally thought of as being the most helpful for students with a verbal IQ of 70 and above, who also possess a systematic, functional expressive communication system with which the student communicates beyond the level of basic wants and needs. Cognitive behavior strategies require meta-cognition, or the ability to think about thinking. These strategies are less effective and may be completely ineffective with students with strong cognitive impairments and/or those who lack the ability to process and respond to sophisticated language-based descriptors.

An equally important characteristic of students for whom social thinking and related social skills instruction is warranted is their level of perspective taking skill, which varies widely across the autism spectrum. This author summarized three hypothetical levels of perspective taking in individuals with ASD (Winner, 2002):

1. Severely Impaired Perspective Taker (SIPT)
2. Emerging Perspective Taker (EPT)
3. Impaired Interactive Perspective Taker (IIPT)

However, these levels, themselves, are on a "spectrum", and many students "blend" across two different levels. Students change rapidly during their preschool and early elementary school years. It is important to avoid determining the perspective taking level of a student before third grade. Additional information that includes a discussion of appropriate treatment strategies for each level can be found in this author's book, *Thinking About YOU Thinking About ME, 2nd Edition* (2007).

As work in the field of social cognition evolves, it will become increasingly important for parents, educators, administrators and politicians to recognize that by uniting all persons with autism, PDD-NOS, Asperger Syndrome, etc. under one semantic umbrella called "autism spectrum disorders" we do an injustice to the highly heterogeneous nature of this population. There is no one singular treatment program that is, or will be, applicable to every person with an autism diagnosis. We currently stress that each individual is unique, and that the characteristics of autism or Asperger Syndrome can manifest in children in an infinite number of permutations. Let us not lose sight of this when considering social thinking and related social skills. Treatment must be tailored to the unique needs of each student.

## Chapter 10

# How Does Social Teaching Fit Into What We Typically Call "Education"?

As readers have come to appreciate by this point, social thinking and related social skills are used throughout the school day, whether a student is working independently, is part of small group or large group instruction in the classroom, is moving from class to class, present during lunch and recess, or participating in extracurricular, school-based activities. Within the confines of the academic curriculum, social thinking skills enable a student to make sense of the curriculum, understand characters and events in current day and historical accounts, and acquire the prerequisite knowledge upon which future class assignments are predicated. There is, then, no place or situation within the school environment where social thinking and related skills are not used.

A natural conclusion, therefore, is that these skills are so germane to any student's education that social teachings should take their rightful place as vital classroom curriculum, and no longer be relegated to only helping children navigate the playground or the lunch break. Instruction about social participation needs to be focused more explicitly in the classroom. The Council for Exceptional Children studied teachers' perceptions of their neurotypical students' social skills in the education classroom. Their conclusion was that social teachings need to be made more explicit across all grade levels for *all* children, not just children with social relational challenges (Lane, Wehby & Cooley, 2006).

This may be popular thought, but the reality falls far from the mark. Query different teachers and school administrators about practices relating to the teaching of social skills, and the majority will respond that social skills should be taught during recess. While recess is certainly an environment that requires on-the-spot social thinking and related skills in a setting not structured by adults, it is only one of many contexts in which we need to teach important social thinking concepts. Given the short amount of time students spend in recess, it can be argued that this is, perhaps, one of the least productive environments within which to focus social skills teaching. The student spends far more time within the classroom setting, in small and larger group learning, on a daily basis. This is where the presence or absence of social thinking skills will most affect student success overall.

From a social perspective, it is our students' ability to adapt to a variety of social contexts that best prepares them for independence and adulthood, and increases their chances of success in our society at large. This is the general message of a book entitled *Self-Regulation in Early Childhood* (Bronson, 2000). In a very literal sense, "education" encompasses far more than academics alone.

Despite a widespread acknowledgement that education goes beyond academics, parents, teachers and schools often butt heads in coming to terms with just what constitutes "education." For instance, many students with significant social cognitive challenges are very academically gifted. They have good verbal expressive abilities and strong IQ scores. They rarely qualify for special education services because of their high IQ, so they sail through certain subjects, while struggling or failing other subjects that require critical social thinking skills. At 15, they may be able to devise brilliant mathematical equations at university level thought, but can't summarize a simple seventh grade reading passage. They find it difficult to organize their time and their assignments, turning in outstanding projects, but days late or off-topic because of poor time-management and other executive functioning skills. Parents of these "bright" students frequently listen as the educational team members acknowledge that the student has a medical diagnosis of Asperger Syndrome, but in the same breath explain that this same student doesn't qualify for educational services because their test scores reveal "no academic problems." From this author's experience working with many adults with social learning challenges, academic test scores are meaningless as indicators of adult success.

It is time for schools and IEP teams everywhere to rethink how we define education and find ways to meet the needs of students who struggle with social thinking impairments. We have failed these students far too long. We can start by redefining education and looking to the support provided by federal legislation in accomplishing this task. For instance, the mission statement for one school district in California is that their students be lifelong learners who are "effective communicators, informed thinkers, self-directed learners, collaborative workers, responsible members of society and information processors." This school is on the right track! Clearly, their mission statement conveys an active appreciation that social thinking and related social skills are part of the daily process we call education and their role is to teach more than academics.

Schools who receive federal education funds (and that's most of them) are bound to uphold certain tenets of education written into law by Congress.

In writing these laws, one aim of Congress was that schools prepare students to become productive citizens and contributing members of our society. This goal is no different for students with special needs; it is a right that applies to everyone, not just our neurotypical students. Teachers and administrators often overlook students who don't have overt needs, and "forget" the fact that special education determinations stem from a two-pronged test.

The Individuals with Disabilities Education Act (IDEA 2004) regulations, at 34 CFR 300.101, state that a "local education authority must provide a free and appropriate public education (FAPE) to a special education student even though the child has not failed or been retained in a course and is passing from grade to grade." For years this legal avenue to help our students with social thinking challenges has been available to us. The trouble is, few education professionals use it!

Congress recognized, in writing this regulation, that education was to be defined in a broader sense than just academics, and that some students, despite academic success, may still need special services. The law outlines a two pronged test to qualify for special education services: 1) does the student have an identified disability and 2) does the student require specialized instruction to address any areas of suspected disability and resulting deficits. Notice the law doesn't say "to succeed academically." This is good news for our students with social cognitive deficits. It means if students have deficits in nonacademic areas (which includes social and functional performance), as noted on an assessment protocol, such as an Adaptive Behavior Scale, their areas of weakness should be addressed within an IEP that contains specific goals and services, regardless of whether they are progressing in the academic curriculum and achieving passing grades.

Social teachings need to be made more explicit across all grade levels for all children, not just children with social relational challenges.

As enlightening as this may be to some parents and educators, there still remain significant challenges in getting appropriate services for students with social cognitive challenges. Helping students learn the vital life lessons that spur them on to adulthood is not nearly as simple as implied in our public policy. Congress passed the No Child Left Behind Act (NCLB) in an effort to bring about better education standards for U.S. children. Missing, however, from this important piece of legislation was a definition of "education" that might guide how we teach our children and achieve "success." This author had the opportunity to ask questions to the panel that helped develop NCLB, and posed to the group: "What is the definition of an education that supports the foundation of NCLB?" They responded by saying there was no definition of an education developed, and instead this exercise was up to each state to take on individually. Going back to her home state of California, and perusing the state education website, there was, in fact, no definition of what an education is or should be; instead it defined that we *educate* students using good teaching practices. Clearly, there is much work to be done in shifting attitudes on the part of those who determine educational services to meet the needs of our students who struggle in nonacademic areas.

So we come back, full circle, to the issue that started this section: how does social teaching fit into our current definitions of "education"? It is a question with no easy answer, but one that must be raised again and again if we are to make any headway in serving our students with social cognitive challenges. Collectively, and individually, educators, service providers and parents must begin to question what they think they know about the world of education, and stop assuming we as a public educational system understand what it means to "educate" our students. We need to encourage our IEP team members to discuss this idea, as well as other commonly used terms or concepts we assume imply good practices. Among these are "mainstreaming", "peer modeling to teach appropriate social behavior", "teaching social skills", etc. While these practices may have their own merits, they all have their own pitfalls. It behooves those of us who work in the field of education to continually question and evaluate our practices, recognize the strengths and weaknesses of the routines we have in place, and stir up the pot from time to time so we are sure that, in the end, our children are achieving the success it is our responsibility to provide them.

## Chapter 11

# What are Evidence-based Practices?

# How Do They Apply to Teaching Social Thinking and Related Social Skills?

**P**rofessionals who set standards for public education and parents alike want our students to grow and learn within an effective, economical and safe environment. We want to know that students are being taught using curriculum and models based on best practices in the field of education. An emphasis on children receiving a "quality education" has been present for centuries. However, with the passage of NCLB in the early 21st century, Congress reaffirmed this basic tenet of education, enacting specific requirements within the law that call for, among other things, practices that, to the maximum extent possible, arise from scientifically based research (SBR). "Evidence-based practices" is the terminology widely used now to describe such teaching methodology that is based on research.

This focus on teaching practices backed by evidence of successful outcomes is an important step towards advancing our knowledge and understanding of the learning styles of persons across the autism spectrum. Their sometimes elusive challenges have spawned a wide variety of treatment programs marketed to parents and educators, often described in slick advertising lingo, promising near-miraculous levels of improvement, some even promising that the child will be "cured" of his autism. Some of these programs have merit; others are questionable, at best. They range from more traditional behavior based programs to more eclectic music and movement therapies, from language/communication CDs and DVDs to swimming with dolphins or wearing bronze bracelets. A host of biomedical and homeopathic remedies are now touted as effective in repairing the biophysical challenges associated with ASD, while various forms of psychotherapies and intensive forms of both behavioral and social cognitive treatments have been created and are being widely advertised within the autism community. While many students are achieving success using one or combinations of therapies, there is little formal research that adheres to scientific protocols behind most of these approaches. The question therefore stands: in a field as young as is our understanding of autism spectrum disorders, and within a population that manifests symptoms on a vast spectrum of ability, how do we adhere to the federal requirement to use evidence-based practices when little evidence exists, other than the anecdotal accounts of parents and educators using these therapies?

SBR means that a single treatment method has been subjected to broad research and extensive evaluation, with studies following specific scientific procedures, in much the same way medications are tested by pharmaceutical companies and the FDA to assess their effectiveness for a group of patients with similar symptoms. And therein lies the crux of the problem when considering SBR for the treatment of individuals with ASD. By their very nature, persons with autism spectrum disorders are not a homogenous group but are, in fact, inherently heterogeneous. There are no neat, defined groups or subgroups with common characteristics that manifest in similar ways upon which research of these various treatments can be studied scientifically. Despite common characteristics, like language impairment, social deficits, odd or repetitive behavior, that define a diagnosis on the spectrum, the ways these challenges manifest from child to child are distinct, unique. Simpson (2005, 2006) argues our public educational policy needs to loosen its definition of what is described as "evidence" if we are ever to have more realistic measures for varying treatments across the autism spectrum.

Zosia Zaks, a parent and herself on the spectrum, probes further into this conundrum of aligning SBR with autism treatments, in the first segment of a six-part article on intervention strategies, which appeared in the Jan-Feb 2008 issue of the *Autism Asperger's Digest*, a national magazine on ASD. In her discussion about research, she beckons our attention to several important issues, including the ethics involved in even conducting such analysis:

> "A major problem is the structure and nature of scientific research itself. For example, how can we standardize entry requirements into a program, a necessity for accurate efficacy rates? We can't say with surety that all children entering a certain intervention program have the same levels of challenge or even the same types of challenges. It would be next to impossible to find 58 children with exactly 22% speech delay, 37% social delay, and 16% repetitive behavior – and then administer treatment X in a standard way for one year, resulting in improvements that can then be tallied like ticks on a yardstick. Furthermore, the 'power' of a study is largely determined by the number of participants. Is it realistic to generalize the results of a study with only 12 participants,

however positive or negative they may be, to the rest of the autism population?

Secondly, defining the categories of behavior that a research project will track is complex as well. Is a child who can't talk but is able to communicate using pictures or signs still considered linguistically challenged? What about a child who hugs his parents and responds to their questions but simultaneously does not engage with anyone else? What set of behaviors or skills should researchers focus on? How can they measure an amount of deficit or improvement for behaviors that are defined in subjective terms?

A third problem involves the types of studies we could conduct. If we want to compare treatments using scientific protocols, technically we would need a control group of autistic children who received no interventions. This would be unethical."

Given the pressures educators and administrators face to use evidence-based research in selecting treatments for students with ASD, where and how do social thinking and related social skills – themselves highly subjective and open to individual interpretation – fit? Is it even *possible* to produce "research" substantiating an area of skill development that exists, to date, without common agreement as to its definition, form and function within this population?

It comes as no surprise, therefore, that little research to date has been undertaken in the area of social skills treatment for individuals with ASD. What research that has been/is being done is generally conducted by the very people who created a specific method in their own efforts to substantiate their work. This hardly replicates the requirement of "scientific research" that the study be conducted by outside, independent entities.

Nonetheless, autism professionals are attempting to explore various treatment methodologies in formal and less-formal ways, looking for any patterns of obvious success or failure that might be applicable to a wider segment of this population. When one study compares and contrasts the findings of several other research studies it is called a "meta-analysis" of the research. Within scientific circles this is considered a "high form" of independent research. But even these studies can be fraught with problems that render the "scientific" findings questionable.

In 2007, Bellini, Peters, Benner & Hopf conducted a meta-analysis of the effectiveness of social skill programs within school settings. The authors included in their analysis 55 single-subject research studies that attempted to teach *any* form of social skills to persons with ASD. These various studies encompassed children aged kindergarten through 12th grade, of various

It is paramount in a world where media headlines are often meant to attract attention and produce sales or website hits, that we continually keep in mind that not all research is "good" research.

functioning levels, using different treatment methodologies that lasted different lengths of time. The results were, naturally, largely inconclusive given the wide disparity of individual, skill level, age and program analyzed. Yet the study, in its opening summary, drew this conclusion: *"The results suggest that social skills interventions have been minimally effective for children with ASD,"* implying we cannot teach "social skills" effectively in schools. Quite a broad pronouncement for a meta-analysis that didn't even represent 1/10th of one percent of the autism population!

The paper also offered some general conclusions that appear to be counterintuitive to those of us who have worked in schools with students across a range of ages, including:

- High school students are more apt to learn from social skills treatments than are preschool students.
- The best place to teach social skills is in the classroom environment, rather than through pull-out services.

The study authors, in the conclusion of this meta-analysis, postulated that our best treatments are those that are individually rather than group designed. At least this one point seems to be on track.

To the woe of many an autism professional dedicated to helping this population gain functional social skills, a press release written by persons other than the study's authors, accompanied the public release of their article. The press release led with this damaging and highly inaccurate title: "Study: Social skills programs for children with autism are largely ineffective." The press release over-generalized the article's findings, and media outlets, as they often do, jumped on, circulating this and other equally damaging headlines in print and on the internet: "Schools' autism programs get failing grade" (Reuters, July 2007); "Social Skills Programs For Children With Autism Are Largely Ineffective, Study Suggests" Science Daily (Jun. 26, 2007).

Unfortunately, educators, parents, service providers and lay people saw these headlines, and by all accounts, considered them "fact." Any school administrator who wants a quick reason not to support social skills teachings in their school was handed the very ammunition needed: a "research study" disproving the effectiveness of social skills treatment programs. Despite follow-up articles and statements that corrected the inaccurate headlines, and more accurately explained the research findings, the damage was done. The lesson: while the emphasis may be on practices grounded in SBR, not all SBR can, nor should be, taken at face value.

It is paramount in a world where media headlines are often meant to attract attention and produce sales or website hits, that we continually keep in mind that not all research is "good" research. Study findings should never be blindly accepted without further investigation of the data and the methods used and a careful reading that analyzes whether or not the data supports the conclusions. It is no longer enough that a research study appear in a peer-reviewed professional journal for professionals and parents to consider it "gospel." Even highly respected journals have acknowledged misprints and post-publication findings of data tampering and misstatements by study authors.

We must begin to ask more sensitive questions when evaluating research being done with this population, questions that acknowledge 1) the diverse range of functioning within individuals with ASD and 2) emerging professional speculation that different treatment methodologies are likely best applied to different segments of the autism spectrum. The Bellini et al (2007) article has taught us that if we ask a question that is not sensitive to the differences across the autism spectrum, our results will also be insensitive and inconclusive. Furthermore, whether we like it or not, media's interest in autism issues grows on a daily basis. Reporters and writers inexperienced with autism are prevalent, and are taking the lead in information sharing. Their reporting can as easily hurt as help the dissemination of accurate information. In the end, the responsibility lies with each of us to fully investigate rather than blindly accept what we read, since their interpretation of our research gets the widest readership of all.

How do we do this? How does a teacher or a parent or a school administrator or a speech therapist assess treatment efficacy, given the different levels and varying profiles of individuals on the autism spectrum? We can start by keeping in mind these points:

1. We have no consensus, national or international, that delineates how we might segment the autism spectrum into different classifications of ability or levels of characteristics upon which research can be based. While this author believes this can be done by assessing different levels of perspective taking skills, many other professionals look to language levels or cognitive functioning as possible profile markers. What this means is that, at this point in our understanding of ASD, we are not able to reach agreement on standard definitions of who has Asperger Syndrome versus who has high-functioning autism, for instance.

2. Treatments for individuals on the autism spectrum should not only be sensitive to the type of autism characteristics manifested, but also the age of the person exhibiting the

**Instead of assessing treatments across the spectrum, we need to focus on analyzing them within the spectrum.**

disability. Thus, we must base decisions or our analysis taking into consideration that preschool learners will respond differently than will school aged students or young adults. Instead of assessing treatments *across* the spectrum, we need to focus on analyzing them *within* the spectrum. Common sense tells us that the physical, social and emotional development of a 4-year old will be substantially different than that of a 17-year old.

3. If we accept that the core nature of ASD is a social-emotional learning disability, (and most experts in the field agree with this), then we must also acknowledge that persons with social challenges experience mental health issues (Abell & Hare, 2005; Bellini, 2004; Farrugia & Hudson, 2006; Hedley & Young, 2006; Stewart, Barnard, Pearson, Hasan, & O'Brien, 2006) that affect their functioning in other areas, particularly individuals with an awareness of what other people think of them. Therefore, despite our desire to group individuals into categories or profiles of ability, effective treatment will always be based on the individual social-emotional needs of the student. To do any less vastly increases the behavior problems exhibited by

students with ASD, from the lowest to the highest functioning. As we attempt to define different treatment methodologies for different levels of the spectrum, this over-riding principle will need to take center stage: a program will only be considered good treatment if it is flexible enough to cater to the presenting student's personal social emotional needs. Those without this component are doomed before they even start.

4. Treatment for persons with ASD can last a lifetime, given the nuance and sophistication of the ever-changing social world and the complexities we encounter as we age. We use faulty logic from the onset when we assume we can measure comprehensive shifts in a student's social skills behavior within the short time periods that characterize most research studies. Not coincidentally, most research is designed to span 8-12 weeks, the length of a school semester, to allow university students to design and carry out studies. Is it realistic to think we can measure change in a student's perspective taking abilities after only 8 weeks of treatment? The answer, of course, is no.

5. Furthermore, social skills behavior is fragile, highly dependent on a person's social emotional coping mechanisms at any point in time. From years of experience working with this population, it has been noted that students may regress at times, even though they are learning valuable new social information and social skills. This "regression" happens not because they aren't "improving" but often because as their social thinking and perspective taking abilities grow, an overwhelming amount of information starts to "make sense",

bringing about a certain level of confusion and anxiety until it can be sorted through and thought about. At times, depression can set in as they begin to understand how different they are from their peers. As students become more socially aware in the realms of school, academics, self-advocacy, friendship and problem solving, they experience far more increasingly complex issues. Progress may not always take an even, upward path. Do we pronounce a program as ineffective because, during the time period of the study, regression occurs? There are too many issues at play for simple judgments like this to occur. We should never underestimate the amount of work it takes our students to learn to think socially, nor the pervasive levels of stress they live within on a daily basis.

**6.** Treatment should take into account various other factors that affect a student's social abilities: level of perspective taking challenges, level of cognitive impairment, language development, sensory processing, mental health challenges and developmental age. Without differentiating for these variables, we reach conclusions that are at best, inconclusive.

In light of the preceding discussion, it is relatively easy to see that requiring evidence-based treatment programs to teach social thinking and related social skills is, in actuality, an impossible quest at present. How can we assess an area – social thinking/social skills – that has never been clearly defined, in a population of individuals – those with ASD and related disabilities – that has no common grouping upon which research can be based? We have put the proverbial cart before the horse in being asked to provide "evidence" for an area that remains highly subjective and open to interpretation in every facet of its application!

Bigger questions loom overhead, questions that are not typically discussed at IEP meetings or among those who steer public education and special education laws:

- How do we define "social skills" in terms that can be measured and controlled?
- What specific skills are to be called "social skills"?
- What short and long term outcomes are we seeking in teaching these skills?
- Can we teach social skills in the absence of social thinking?
- What is the goal of social skills treatment? Are we expecting to "cure" ASD or help a student improve their ability to process and respond to social information, compared to their baseline abilities?
- How do we define "mastery" of skills that change and evolve as children age and mature?

However, the time has come to address these questions, and others, if we expect to make any headway in providing "education" to students with ASD and related social cognitive challenges. Never before has the incidence of autism been higher; it grows with each passing year in proportions that approach a national emergency. The Centers for Disease Control, in mid-2007, released their latest autism figures. Nationally, autism occurs in 1 in every 150 students. In some states that figure is as high as 1 in every 96 children. While this statistic is widely circulated, what our society fails to appreciate is that these are figures generated as a result of school census taken in 2000-2002. *These figures are already 5 years old*, and in all likelihood, autism affects far more children than we are even considering. When we pair this explosive need for education and services with a more intensely defined national educational policy focused on evidence-based practices, we find public agencies stymied, unable to act because there is no clear indication of where to go or how to get there! Many administrators draw the line in the sand: unless there is evidence to support the teaching of social skills, there will be no social skills teaching programs in the school, neglecting to even undertake an investigation into the issue to determine if this mandate is even possible. In fact, this author was motivated to write this paper by the growing number of special education directors calling, all asking the same question: "What evidence-based social skills teaching programs are available to use in our school?" The interest in providing students with programs to address their social deficits is alive within our community. What remains unattended to are the questions that must be asked – and answered – before evidence-based practices can be created to meet these needs.

Until these more global discussions take place, as a community of parents and educators we must use caution when deciding "best practices" for teaching individual students social thinking and related social skills. As we do so, let's assure we are not making educational decisions for each student based on a "PEP" (political educational policy), rather than on an IEP (individual education plan) that respects the unique and diverse needs of this population as a whole.

## Rethinking and reframing evidence-based teachings

Virtually all professionals will attest: teaching social thinking and related social skills is virgin territory within the larger community of individuals responsible for the education and care of individuals with ASD and other social thinking challenges. As mentioned at the beginning of this paper, professionals who have spent the most time exploring the concept of social functioning have done so in fields unrelated to ASD: cultural and evolutionary anthropology, cultural linguistics, sociology, etc.

Those of us within the autism community with an interest in exploring these more global questions related to social thinking and social skills are still feeling our way around in largely uncharted territory, stepping into the role of pioneers in mapping out a new world of understanding in autism. It's an exciting venture, for sure.

The good news is that explorers have gone before us, leaving a bumpy trail that offers some direction. There are professionals in various areas of expertise who have already considered what it means to use evidence-based teaching methods. They do not all concur on one formal definition. In fact, what constitutes "evidence-based practices" varies among different arms of treatment professionals. Behaviorists tend to adhere to the definition of evidence-based practices as those arising from "scientifically rigorous" research completed according to formal research protocols. Allied health professionals (psychologists, counselors, occupational therapists, speech language pathologists, etc.), on the other hand, define evidence-based practices as those which "recognize the needs, abilities, values, preferences, and interests of individuals and families to whom they provide clinical services, and integrate those factors along with best current research evidence and their clinical expertise in making clinical decisions" (ASHA, 2005, p. 1). Behaviorists want to see hard data that supports a teaching methodology. Allied health professionals seem to take into consideration that not all aspects of functioning can be objectively defined, tested and measured, and that "success" is dependent on many internal and external variables, all working in concert with each other. This disparity in defining evidence-based practice only goes to reinforce that we in the fledgling stages of understanding and reaching consensus on this term and how it should be applied within our education system. Clearly further discussion is warranted.

Within the realm of teaching students with social learning challenges, it is the allied health professionals' definition that gives us a fighting chance to discover practices that can be used successfully. Social thinking instruction involves treatment that explores not only social communication but complex social emotional responses. If our goal is to determine the "best or most promising" practices, we need to consider more than the best scientific evidence. Social skills play out in the "real world", one that involves family/client values, cultural differences, economic backgrounds, not to mention the clinician's experience in the field itself, and any preconceptions and perceptions that clinician brings to the experience.

## A starting point for treatment

Despite the global questions on social thinking and related social skills we have yet to discuss and reach consensus upon, there do exist professionally-developed teaching methods that can be used with students with autism or Asperger Syndrome who are "higher functioning" and have some demonstrated level of Theory of Mind and perspective taking skills. These best practices use cognitive behavioral techniques steeped in developmental knowledge coupled with behavioral teaching practices based on research evidence, together applied within a context that takes into account the individual strengths and weaknesses of the specific student with social learning disabilities (Winner, 2000; Prizant et al, 2006b). When treatment is approached in this way, we begin to notice that methodology does exist that supports our goal to teach students social thinking and related social skills. Effective strategies arise from several sources: naturalistic behavioral treatment techniques (Koegel, 1999), social-emotional strategies a part of the SCERTS model (Prizant et al), relational therapies (Wolfberg, 2003; Greenspan/DIR, 2003; Gutstein/RDI, 2001), Social Stories™ (Gray, 2002) or Social Behavior Mapping and other social thinking and related social skills (Winner, 2007). Which strategies we use, and in what combination, is highly dependent on the profile of the student and family, taking into account their unique needs in their current educational context.

The overall concept of teaching "social thinking and related social skills" is not uniquely tied to the work of one author. Many professionals whose work spills over into this area understand the pivotal role social thinking and social skills play in the overall success of the individual challenged by ASD. The philosophy and basic treatment tenets mentioned above are shared by many other pioneering therapy professionals in the field of ASD (Gray, 2002, Attwood, 2007, Wolfberg, 2003, Myles, Trautman & Schelvan, 2004, Arwood & Kaulitz, 2007). However, the primary work of this author has been solely in the field of social thinking and related social skills for over two decades. And, it is encouraging that this work is beginning to attract the attention of independent researchers. A preliminary research study is presently underway to evaluate some of this author's specific techniques in teaching social thinking to students on the higher functioning end of the autism spectrum. Crooke, Hendrix and Rachman (2007) demonstrated positive treatment/generalization effects with a small group, single subject design exploring social thinking treatment. Elementary-aged boys were taught social thinking concepts such as "expected/unexpected", "think with your eyes" and "listen with your whole body" in a small group therapeutic setting. Robust gains in both

The success of any treatment method is largely dependent on the quality of the person offering the treatment.

skills and generalization of skills were demonstrated when the boys were placed in a new setting, a pizza party. Their research supports the theory that if we teach students to think socially they can take their thinking and use it effectively outside the therapy room.

## The role of the teacher

No discussion of evidence-based practice is complete without considering the role the teacher plays in the outcome of any therapeutic program. Behavior doesn't occur within a vacuum, and it is common knowledge within the community of autism and behavior therapy that behavior arises from the interaction of a child and his environment. That environment includes the people in it, including the teacher.

Interestingly, the SBR evidence-based practice movement curiously omits of the role of the professional and/or paraprofessional and even the parent as a critical component in any successful treatment program. Scientific data can be compelling, but does not necessarily provide evidence of "good teaching" when students are required to learn information through the presentation of other people. In a nutshell the point being made is this: the success of any treatment method is largely dependent on the quality of the person offering the treatment.

Many articles have been penned to date about the "art and science" of teaching (e.g., Fey & Fey, 2004; Bernstein, 2006; Kent, 2006). Effective education does more than teach "facts" to students. The role of the teacher is to instill a joy in learning in our children, and provide students with skills that allow them to achieve success as they continue to learn outside the classroom. Test scores are only a small part of what it means to "get an education." Therefore, the value of an experienced parent or professional, one who can make spontaneous judgment calls in a problematic situation or recognize when learning is at a standstill and shift gears as needed, is not to be underscored or omitted from our discussions of SBR methods. Certainly parents, educators and education administrators recognize that a "good teacher" trumps scientific data any day. SBR alone will never assure success in teaching students to become successful adults.

What qualities distinguish an educator who is most apt to achieve success in teaching children with challenges in social thinking and related social skills? In 2007, this author had the opportunity to lead a team discussion of school-based professionals in Orange County, California, who work with students with Asperger Syndrome and like disabilities. The goal was to explore "best teachings" in light of the "art" and "science" of teaching. The group defined the "art" as teaching dynamically by:

- Being flexible to the student's needs
- Choosing goals that meet and support the needs of the student and the team's focus
- Taking advantage of teachable moments
- Being able to monitor the "macro" and "micro" aspects of education
- Teaching at the child's pace
- Developing social emotional rapport with the student
- Understanding how to group kids to foster maximum learning
- Applying calm, consistent discipline based on behavior management principles
- Earning the trust of the student
- Considering the student's and family's values

Student and family values are often overlooked and underappreciated in assessing the various treatment methods. Yet, they are a basic component of program development and contribute significantly to program success or failure. Teachers have limited contact with a student, and teaching social thinking and social skills is a 24/7 endeavor. The need to practice these skills does not stop once the student leaves school each day. Parents, therefore, play a critical role in treatment success. How they view the program, whether they feel skilled in reinforcing goals and objectives at home or in the community can motivate or deter them from supporting the teacher's lessons. And, the motivation of the student to expend the huge effort that social understanding requires is paramount to success. A student who doesn't enjoy this learning, or can't perceive the value it may have for him, will likely be uninterested in doing the necessary work, either in school or outside school.

The social thinking approach described in this article has been actively taught at the clinic this author founded in California and by other treatment providers around the country since 1998. As part of our own measures to gauge treatment success, parents are regularly surveyed. This does not formally meet the definition of SBR, but does provide anecdotal evidence about the treatment methods used. In 2006, 40 parents responded to a survey of services; 100% reported positive results for their children. A vast percentage of parents mentioned the helpfulness of the social thinking vocabulary concepts, which gave parents a tool to teach their child to self-monitor behavior at home and opened up opportunities for family discussions about social processing and social expectations. The parents of a 45-year-old woman with high-functioning autism and a history of behavior problems, wrote to say the program has given them "hope that her life can improve...for the first time their daughter has started to modify her own behavior. She is more controlled, less hostile and makes more of an effort to express an interest in other people's activities."

The social thinking approach encourages students to more actively consider and process social information around them as a prerequisite to making a social (skills) response, i.e., think socially before acting socially. Students are, at times, asked to make journal entries to explain how their social thinking program has helped them cope in their communities. Two teenaged boys in a social thinking high school program in an eastern state wrote journal entries six months into their treatment programs to answer this prompted question: "How do you use social thinking in other places or times outside of the Social Thinking Center?" A sample of their responses follows:

> "At home, at parties, in all sorts of places. I look around and see what others are doing, and then if I'm doing something unexpected or different I'll ask them to do something with me."

> "Anywhere when I am trying to understand people when they're being confusing….whenever people are being confusing which unfortunately is kinda often."

A 12-year-old boy who has worked with this author for three years, summarized what he learned this year at our clinic:

> "I finally got it that people think about me all the time whether I want them to or not, so I have to monitor my behavior all the time whether I want to or not."

Quite a social revelation!

## Chapter 12

# We End at the Beginning

T he concept of teaching "social skills" misrepresents the dynamic and complex process that is at the heart of social skill production. Before we can act socially, we need to be able to think socially. Professionals in fields such as evolutionary anthropology, cultural linguistics and sociology have spent generations studying the complex nature of social development in man and society. However, this is an area of new exploration within the realm of educators and clinicians.

Our education system is built upon certain assumptions about the social development of children. Educators assume that children enter school-aged programs with a "social operating system" that has been progressively "teaching" the child, through mostly intuitive means, since birth. School-based lessons are predicated on the assumption that by the time the child enters public school, certain basic social skills are ingrained: skills that allow children to attend, learn, gain access to groups, and blend in from a social behavioral perspective with their peers. However, students with social learning challenges, most commonly represented by students with ASD, have faulty brain wiring that precludes the natural social operating system from functioning, to greater or lesser degrees. These individuals need to learn cognitively social information their peers have gleaned intuitively, social information that to date has not been woven into our current definition of education or the standards that support it.

Special education law (IDEA 2004) stipulates students need to learn social as well as academic information as part of their educational programs. Public educational policy, specifically the No Child Left Behind Act, has ushered in a new focus on using scientifically based research (SBR) in choosing specific teaching methodologies. However, the disparate nature of these two mandates has resulted in confusion within the ranks of teachers and administrators everywhere. Questions loom large and go largely unanswered: "What evidence exists to support teaching social skills programs?", "Which program models are backed with SBR?", "How do we define social skills in light of evidence-based practices?"

The answers to these questions are complex and we are in our infancy in exploring them. To date, education professionals have responded to the call for social skills instruction by using concrete behavioral techniques. While this has proven relatively effective for our "lower functioning" or "cognitive impaired" student population, this type of instruction is grossly insufficient for addressing the more cognitive behavioral learning needs of students who demonstrate mild to severe social learning challenges, yet have near normal to above normal intelligence and verbal expressive skills. These bright, but socially inept students, need to be taught to think socially as a precursor to them learning appropriate social actions.

This exploration into social thinking and social skills poses 10 critical questions that explore the dynamic nature of the social behavioral response we describe as "social skills" and the underlying thoughts and perceptions that support these skills. The fact that we have put the "cart before the horse", requesting and requiring social skill treatment methodologies that are "evidence-based" before we have fully understood the dynamic and synergistic nature of what constitutes "social skills" is fully discussed. A call to action is made, one that challenges us to recognize we have yet to reach consensus on basic definitions in this emerging field of study, and to actively engage in discussions that illuminate the pivotal role that social thinking plays in not just academics, but all areas of education, inside and outside the school environment.

As logic prevails, it is recognized there is more than one type of "evidence-based practice" and that educators, administrators and parents should continue to value not only the "best scientific evidence available" but also other factors that have a direct influence on the success or failure of any instruction method: student and family values, cultural and environmental issues, preconceptions towards treatment, the expertise in understanding and treating social thinking and social challenges of the professional delivering instruction, as well as the "art" teachers bring to the teaching experience.

The paramount purpose of this article is to encourage those adults who work and live with persons with ASD and other social learning challenges to think more deeply about the lessons we are teaching our students, at school, at home and in the community. Instruction that neglects to take into account the complex nature of social thinking and social skills disrespects our students and sets up a cycle of repeated failure, rather than ongoing success. Programs that achieve the success we hope for these students start by asking certain fundamental questions, without judgment or preconceptions about the student's level of functioning or need: "What are social skills?", "How do we teach them to a student in light of his individual presentation of strengths and weaknesses?" and more importantly, "How can we teach deeper social thinking skills as the foundation of a comprehensive effort to bring about social understanding in our higher functioning students?"

Finally, we must acknowledge that social thinking and social skills are fluid, changing, responsive skills, dependent upon factors internal and external to the student. Our programs must be equally fluid and responsive, guided by teachers who possess the innate personality and social curiosity that allow them to step outside conventional teaching curriculum and explore new avenues of social instruction that are meaningful and motivating to these students. In doing so, we expand our current idea of "education" to encompass instruction geared not just to students who present with neurotypically developing social systems, but to *all* students. That is, in the long run, a worthy goal indeed.

# Bibliography

Abell, F. & Hare, D. (2005). An experimental investigation of the phenomenology of delusional beliefs in people with Asperger Syndrome. *Autism*. Vol. 9 (5), December 2005. 515-532.

Adolphs, R. (2003). Investigating the cognitive neuroscience of social behavior. *Neuropsychologia, 41*, 119-126.

Allman, W. (1995a). *The Stone Age Present*. New York: Simon and Schuster.

Allman, W. (1995b). *Storming the Citadel. In: The Stone Age Present*. New York: Simon and Schuster, chapter 1, page 36.

American Psychiatric Association (2000). *Diagnostic and Statistical Manual of Mental Disorders* (4th ed., text rev.) Washington, DC: Author.

American Speech-Language-Hearing Association (2005). Evidence-based practice in communication disorders (position paper). Available at: http://www.asha.org/members/deskreferjournals/deskref/default. (pp1)

Anderson, S., & Morris, J. (2006). Cognitive behavior therapy for people with Asperger syndrome. *Behavioural and Cognitive Psychotherapy, 34* (3), 293-303.

anthropology. (n.d.). *Dictionary.com Unabridged (v 1.0.1)*. Retrieved September 25, 2006, from Dictionary.com website: http://dictionary.reference.com/browse/anthropology

Arwood, E. & Kaulitz, C. (2007) *Learning With a Visual Brain in an Auditory World*. Visual language strategies for individuals with autism spectrum disorders. Autism Asperger Publishing, Shawnee, Kansas.

Aspy, R. & Grossman, B. (2007) *The Ziggurat Model. A Framework For Designing Comprehensive Interventions For Individuals With High Functioning Autism And Asperger Syndrome*. Autism Asperger Publishing Co. Shawnee Mission, Kansas.

Association of California School Administrators. (2003). *Handbook Of Goals And Objectives Related To Essential State Of California Content Standards*. ACSA: California.

Attwood, T. (1998). *Asperger Syndrome. A Guide For Parents And Professionals*. Pennsylvania: Jessica Kingsley Publishers.

Attwood, T. (2003). Cognitive Behavior Therapy (CBT). In L.H. Willey (Ed.) *Asperger Syndrome In Adolescence. Living With The Ups And Downs And Things In Between*. Pennsylvania: Jessica Kingsley Publishers.

Attwood, T. (2007). *The Complete Guide To Asperger Syndrome*. Pennsylvania: Jessica Kingsley Publishers.

Ayres, J. (1979). *Sensory Integration And The Child*. Los Angeles: Western Psychological Services.

Baron-Cohen, S. (2000). Theory of mind and autism: a fifteen year review. In S. Baron-Cohen, H. Tager-Flusberg. and D. Cohen (Eds.), *Understanding Other Minds: Perspectives From Developmental Cognitive Neuroscience*. New York: Oxford University Press.

Baron-Cohen, S., Baldwin, D.A., & Crowson, M. (1997). Do children with autism use the speaker's direction of gaze strategy to crack the code of language? *Child Development, 68*, 48-57.

Baron-Cohen, S. Jollife, T., Mortimore, C. & Robertson, M. (1997). Another advanced test of theory of mind: Evidence from very high functioning adults with autism or Asperger Syndrome. *Journal of Child Psychology and Psychiatry, 38*, No.7, 813-822.

Baron-Cohen, S. (1995). *Mindblindness: An Essay On Autism And Theory Of Mind*. Cambridge, MA: MIT Press.

Baron-Cohen, S., Leslie, A.M. & Frith, U. (1985). Does the autistic child have a "theory of mind?" *Cognition, 21*, 37-46.

Beaumont, R. & Newcombe, P. (2006). Theory of mind and central coherence in adults with high-functioning autism or Asperger Syndrome. *Autism*. Vol. 10 (4), 365-382.

Beebe, D., & Risi, S. (2003). Treatment of adolescents and young adults with high-functioning autism and Asperger syndrome. In M. Reinecke, F. Dattilio, & A. Freeman (Eds.), *Cognitive therapy and adolescents: A casebook for clinical practice*, 2nd edition (pp. 369-401). New York, NY: Guilford Press.

Bellini, S. (2004). Social skill deficits and anxiety in high functioning adolescent with autism spectrum disorders. *Focus on Autism and Other Developmental Disabilities*, Vol. 19 (2), 78-86.

Bellini, S., Peters, J., Benner, L., & Hopf, A. (2007). A meta-analysis of school-based social skills interventions for children with autism spectrum disorders".*Journal of Remedial and Special Education. 28* (3), 153-162.

Bernstein Ratner, N. (2006). Evidence-based practice: An examination of its ramifications for the practice of Speech-Language Pathology. Language, Speech and Hearing in Schools, *ASHA*, Vol. 37, 257-267.

Bloom, L. (1998) Research Perspectives: Language Development and Emotional Expression. Pediatrics, Vol. 102 No. 5 Supplement 1998, pp 1272-1277.

Bondy, A. and Frost, L. (2002) A Picture's Worth: PECS and other visual communication strategies in autism. Topics in autism. Woodbine House: Bethesda, MD.

Bronson, M. (2000). *Self-Regulation In Early Childhood.* New York: The Guilford Press.

Brown, G. & Yule, G. (1983). *Discourse Analysis.* Cambridge, U.K.: Cambridge University Press.

Buron, K. (2007). *A 5 is Against the Law! Social Boundaries Straight Up!* Shawnee Mission, KS: Autism Asperger Publishing Company.

Buron, K. D., & Curtis, M. (2003). *The Incredible 5-Point Scale.* Shawnee Mission, KS: Autism Asperger Publishing Company.

Crooke, P.J., Hendrix, R.E., Rachman, J.Y., (2007). Brief Report: Measuring the effectiveness of teaching social thinking to children with Asperger Syndrome (AS) and High Functioning Autism (HFA). *Journal of Autism and Developmental Disorders,* Online publication: DOI 10.1007/s10803-007-0466-1

De Villiers, J. (2000). Language and theory of mind: what are the developmental relationships? In S. Baron-Cohen, H. Tager-Flusberg. & D. Cohen (Eds.), *Understanding other minds. Perspectives from Developmental Cognitive Neuroscience.* New York: Oxford University Press.

Dobson, K. & Dozois, D. (2001). Historical and philosophical bases of the cognitive-behavioral therapies. In K. Dobson, *Handbook of Cognitive Behavioral Therapies.* New York: The Guilford Press.

Eslinger, P.J. (1996). Conceptualizing, describing and measuring components of executive function: A summary. In G.R. Lyon & N.A. Krasnegor (Eds.), *Attention, Memory and Executive Function* (pp.367-395). Baltimore: Brookes.

Farrugia, S. & Hudson, J. (2006). Anxiety in adolescents with Asperger Syndrome: Negative thoughts, behavioral problems and life interference. *Focus on Autism and Other Developmental Disabilities,* Vol. 21 (1), 25-35.

Fey, L.M. & Fey, M.E. (2004, Sept 21). Evidence-based practice in schools: Integrating craft and theory with science and data. *The ASHA Leader,* pp.4-5, 30-32.

Field, T.M., Cohen, D., Garcia, R., & Collins, R. (1983). Discrimination and imitation of facial expressions by term and preterm neonates. *Infant Behavior and Development, 6,* 485-489.

Frith, U. (1989). *Autism. Explaining the Enigma.* Massachusetts: Basil Blackwell, Inc.

Fullerton, A., Stratton, J., Coyne, P., & Gray, C. (1996). *Higher Functioning Adolescents And Young Adults With Autism.* Austin, Texas: Pro-ED, Inc.

Gardner, H. (1993). *Multiple Intelligences. The Theory In Practice.* New York: Basic Books, pg 29.

Gaylord-Ross, R.J., Haring, T.G., Breen, C. & Pitts-Conway, V. (1984). The training and generalization of social interaction skills with autistic youth. *Journal of Applied Behavior Analysis, 17*(2), 229-47.

Goleman, D. (1995). *Emotional Intelligence.* New York, NY: Bantam Books.

Goleman, D. (2006). *Social Intelligence: The New Science Of Social Relationships.* New York: Bantam Books.

Gopnik, A., Meltzoff, A. & Kuhl, P. (1999). *The Scientist In The Crib.* New York: Harper Perennial.

Gray, C. (1994). *Comic Strip Conversations.* Arlington, TX: Future Horizons Publishers.

Gray, C. (2002). *My Social Stories Book.* Philadelphia, PA: Jessica Kingsley Publishers.

Greenspan, S. & Wieder, S. (2003). *Engaging Autism: The Floortime Approach To Helping Children Relate, Communicate And Think.* Jackson, TN: Perseus Books. www.perseusbooksgroup.com.

Grice, H. P. (1975). Logic and conversation. In P. Cole (Ed.) *Syntax and Semantics.* Vol. 3, 41-58. New York: Academic Press.

Gutstein, S.E. (2001). *Autism/Aspergers: Solving The Relationship Puzzle.* Arlington, TX: Future Horizons.

Happe, F. (1994). An advanced test of theory of mind: Understanding the story characters thoughts and feelings by able autistic mentally handicapped and normal children and adults. *Journal of Autism & Developmental Disorders, 24,* 129-154.

Happe, F. (1994). *Autism And Introduction To Psychological Theory.* Massachusetts: Harvard University Press.

Hedley, D. & Young, R. (2006). Social comparison processes and depressive symptoms in children and adolescents with Asperger Syndrome. *Autism.* Vol.10 (2), 139-153.

Henry, S. & Myles, B. (2007) *The Comprehensive Autism Planning System (Caps) For Individuals With Asperger Syndrome, Autism And Related Disabilities: Integrating Best Practices Throughout The Student's Day.* Autism Asperger Publishing Company, Shawnee, Kansas.

Hirsh-Pasek, K., Golinkoff, R. & Eyer, D. (2003a). *Einstein Never Used Flash Cards.* Rodale Press.

Hirsh-Pasek, K., Golinkoff, R. & Eyer, D. (2003b). Play the Crucible of Learning, in *Einstein Never Used Flash Cards.* Rodale Press. Pp 205-243.

Howlin, P & Yates, P. (1999). The potential effectiveness of social skills group for adults with autism. *Autism*, 3, 299-307.

Hoyt, L. (1999). *Revisit, Reflect And Retell. Strategies For Improving Reading Comprehension.* New Hampshire: Heinemann.

Ihrig, K., & Wolchik, S.A. (1988). Peer versus adult models and autistic children's learning: Acquisition, generalization and maintenance. *Journal of Autism and Developmental Disorders, 18* (1) 67-79.

Individuals with Disabilities Education Improvement Act of 2004, Pub. L. 108-446. 34 C.F.R. 300.101.

Jones, E. &. Carr, E.G. (2004). Joint attention in children with autism: Theory and intervention. *Focus on Autism and Other Developmental Disabilities,* 19 (1), 13-26.

Kanner, L. (1943). Autistic disturbances of affective contact. *Nervous Child, 2,* 217-250.

Kent, R. (2006). Evidence-based practice in communication disorders: Progress not perfection. Language, Speech and Hearing in Schools, *ASHA*, Vol 37, 268-270.

Koegel, L.K., and R.L. Koegel (1999a). Pivotal response intervention I: Overview of approach. *Journal of the Association for the Severely Handicapped,* 24:174-185. [148]

Krantz, P. & McClannahan, L. (1993). Teaching children with autism to initiate to peers: Effects of a script-fading procedure. *Journal of Applied Behavior Analysis, 26,* 121-132.

Kuhlmeier, V; Wynn, K. & Bloom, P. (2003). Attribution of dispositional states by 12-month olds. *Psychological Science,* Volume 14, issue 5, pp 402-408.

Kunce, L. & Mesibov, G. (1998). Educational approaches to High-Functioning Autism and Asperger Syndrome (Chapter 11). In Schopler, E., Mesibov, G. & Kunce, L, *Asperger Syndrome or High-Functioning Autism?* New York: Plenum Press.

Lane, K., Wehby, J. & Cooley, C. (2006). Teacher expectations of students' classroom behavior across the grade span: Which social skills are necessary for success? *Council for Exceptional Children.* Vol 72 (2), 153-167.

Levine, M. (2002). *A Mind At A Time.* New York: Simon & Schuster.

Linguistics. (n.d.). *Dictionary.com Unabridged (v 1.0.1).* Retrieved October 13, 2006, from Dictionary.com website: http://dictionary.reference.com/browse/Linguistics

Lord, C. (1993). The complexity of social behavior in autism. In S. Baron-Cohen, H. Tager-Flusberg, & D. Cohen (Eds.), *Understanding Other Minds: Perspectives From Autism* (pp. 292-316). Oxford, England: Oxford University Press.

Lovaas, O. I. (1987). Behavioral treatment and normal intellectual and educational functioning in autistic children. *Journal of Consulting and Clinical Psychology, 55,* 3-9.

Marans, W.D., Rubin, E. & Laurent, A. (2005). Addressing social communication skills in individuals with high functioning autism and Asperger Syndrome; Critical priorities in educational programming. In F.R. Volkmar, A. Klin, & R. Paul (Eds.), *Handbook Of Autism And Pervasive Developmental Disorders (Third Edition).* New York: John Wiley.

Marshall, P. & Fox, N.(Eds.). (2006). The development of social engagement. *Neurobiological Perspectives.* New York: Oxford University Press.

McEvoy, R., Rogers, S. & Pennington, B. (1993). Executive Function and social communication deficits in young autistic children. *Journal of Child Psychology and Psychiatry, 32* (4), 563-578.

Meltzoff, A.N. (1995) Understanding intentions of others: re-enactment of intended acts by 18-month-old children. *Developmental Psychology, 31* (5) 838-850.

Miller, L., Gillam, R. & Pena, E. (2001). *Dynamic Assessment And Intervention: Improving Children's Narrative Abilities.* Texas: Pro-Ed, Inc.

Minshew, N., Goldstein, G., Muenz. L., & Payton, J. (1992). Neuropsychological functioning in non-mentally retarded autistic individuals. *Journal of Clinical and Experimental Neuropsychology, 14,* (5), 749-761.

Mundy, P. & Crowson, M. (1997). Joint attention and early social communication: implications for research on intervention with autism. *Journal of Autism and Developmental Disorders,* Vol. 27, No. 6, 653-676.

Myles, B., Cook, K., Miller, N., Rinner, L., and Robbins, L. (2000). *Asperger Syndrome And Sensory Issues. Practical Solutions For Making Sense Of The World.* Kansas: Autism Asperger Publishing Company.

Myles, B. Trautman, M., Schelvan, R. (2004). *The Hidden Curriculum: Practical Solutions For Understanding Unstated Rules In Social Situations.* Kansas: Autism Asperger Publishing Company.

No Child Left Behind Act of 2001, Pub. L. 107-110. 20 U.S.C. 70 §6301 et seg.

Ozonoff, S. & Griffith, E. (2000). Neuropsychological function and the external validity of Asperger Syndrome. In Klin. A., Volkmar, F., & Sparrow, S., (Eds.), *Asperger Syndrome.* New York: The Guilford Press.

Parish, P. (1977). *Teach Us, Amelia Bedelia.* Scholastic, New York, NY.

Perner, J., Frith, U., Leslie, A. M., & Leekam, S. R. (1989). Exploration Of The Autistic Child's Theory Of Mind: Knowledge, Belief, And Communication. *Child Development, 60,* 689-700.

Perry, A. & Condillac, R. (2003). *Evidence-Based Practices For Children And Adolescents With Autism Spectrum Disorders: Review Of The Literature And Practice Guide.* Ontario: Children's Mental Health

Prelock, P. (2006). *Autism Spectrum Disorders. Issues In Assessment And Intervention.* Texas. Pro-ED, Inc.

Prior, M., Dahlstrom, B., & Squires, T. L. (1990). Autistic children's knowledge of thinking and feeling in other people. *Journal of Child Psychology & Psychiatry, 31,* 587-601.

Prizant, B.; Wetherby, A. & Rydell, P. (2000) Communication Intervention Issues for Children with Autism Spectrum Disorders. Wetherby, A. and Prizant, B (eds) *Autism Spectrum Disorders: A Transactional Developmental Perspective,* Volume 9. Paul H. Brooks Publishing Company, Baltimore, Maryland.

Prizant, B., Wetherby, A., Rubin, E., Laurent, A. & Rydell, P. (2006a). *The SCERTS™ Model. A Comprehensive Educational Approach For Children With Autism Spectrum Disorders. Volume II Program Planning and Intervention.* Maryland: Brookes Publishing.

Prizant, B., Wetherby, A., Rubin, E., Laurent, A. & Rydell, P. (2006b). *The SCERTS™ Model. A Comprehensive Educational Approach For Children With Autism Spectrum Disorders. Volume 1, Assessment.* Maryland: Brookes Publishing.

Reynhout, G., & Carter, M. (2006). Social Stories™ for children with disabilites. *Journal of Autism and Developmental Disorders.* Vol 36 (4), 445-469.

Russel, J. (1997). *Autism As An Executive Disorder.* New York: Oxford University Press.

Sabbagh, M. (2006). Neurocognitive bases of preschooler's theory of mind development: Integrating cognitive neuroscience and cognitive development. In Marshall, P. & Fox, N. (Eds.), *The Development Of Social Engagement: Neurobiological Perspectives.* New York: Oxford University Press.

Shah, A. & Frith, U. (1993). Why do autistic individuals show superior performance on the block design task? *Journal of Child Psychology and Psychiatry, 34*, (8), 1351-1364.

Simmons-Mackie, N. & Damico, J. (2003). Contributions of qualitative research to the knowledge base of normal communication. *American Journal of Speech Language Pathology,* Vol 12, 144-154.

Simpson, R. (2005). *Autism Spectrum Disorders: Interventions And Treatments For Children And Youth.* California: Corwin Press.

Simpson, R. (2006). Evidence-based practices and students with Autism Spectrum Disorders. *Focus on Autism and Other Developmental Disabilities*, 20 (3), 140-149.

sociology. (n.d.). *Dictionary.com Unabridged (v 1.0.1).* Retrieved September 25, 2006, from Dictionary.com website: http://dictionary.reference.com/browse/sociology

Sofronoff, K., Attwood, T., & Hinton, S. (2005). A randomized controlled trial of a CBT intervention for anxiety in children with Asperger Syndrome. *Journal of Child Psychology and Psychiatry*, 46(11), 1152-1160.

Stewart, M., Barnard, L., Pearson, J., Hasan, R. & O'Brien, G. (2006). Presentation of depression in autism and Asperger Syndrome: a review. *Autism*, Vol. 10 (1), 103-116.

Tager-Flusberg, H. (1999a). A psychological approach to understanding the social and language impairments in autism. *International Review of Psychiatry*, 11, pp 325-334.

Tager-Flusberg, H. (1999b). Language development in atypical children. In M. Barrett (Ed.) *The Development of Language* (pp 311-348). East Sussex, England: Psychology Press.

Tager-Flusberg, H. (2000). Language and Understanding Other Minds: connections in autism. In S. Baron-Cohen, H. Tager-Flusberg. and D. Cohen (Eds.), *Understanding Other Minds: Perspectives From Developmental Cognitive Neuroscience.* New York: Oxford University Press. Pp124-149.

Toplis, R. & Hadwin, J. (2006). Using social stories to change problematic lunchtime behavior in school. *Educational Psychology in Practice,* Vol 22(1), 53-67.

Tovani, C. (2000). *I Read It But I Don't Get It: Comprehension Strategies For Adolescent Readers*. Maine: Stenhouse Publishers.

Twatchman-Cullen, D. (2000). More able children with autism spectrum disorders: Social-communicative challenges and guidelines for enhancing abilities. In A.M. Wetherby and B.M. Prizant (Eds.), *Autism Spectrum Disorders: A Transactional Developmental Approach* (pp. 225-249). Baltimore: Brookes.

Volkmar, F. R. (1987). Social development. In D. J. Cohen and A. M. Donnellan (Eds.), *Handbook of Autism And Pervasive Developmental Disorders* (pp. 41-60). New York: John Wiley & Sons.

Volkmar, F.R., & Klin, A. (1990). Social development in autism: Historical and clinical perspectives. In S. Baron-Cohen, H. Tager-Flusberg, & D. Cohen (Eds.), *Understanding Other Minds: Perspectives From Autism* (pp. 40-55). Oxford, England: Oxford University Press.

Walker, A.S. (1982). Intermodal perception of expressive behaviors by human infants. *Journal of Experimental Child Psychology, 33*, 514-535.

Wellman, H.M. (1990). *The Child's Theory of Mind*. Cambridge, MA: Bradford Books, MIT Press.

Williams, M., & Shellenberger, S. (1996). *How Does Your Engine Run? A Leader's Guide To The Alert Program For Self-Regulation*. Albuquerque, NM: Therapy Works.

Winner, M. G. (2000). *Inside Out: What Makes The Person With Social Cognitive Deficits Tick?* San Jose, CA: Think Social Publishing, Inc. www.socialthinking.com

Winner, M. G. (2002). *Thinking About You Thinking About Me*. San Jose, CA: Think Social Publishing, Inc. www.socialthinking.com

Winner, M. G. (2004). A proposal for a perspective taking spectrum. A new way to understand persons with social-cognitive deficits. *The Educational Therapist*, Vol. 25 (1), 6-13.

Winner, M. G. (2005). *Think Social: A Social Thinking Curriculum For School Age Students*. San Jose, CA: Think Social Publishing, Inc. www.socialthinking.com

Winner, M. G. (2007a). *Thinking About You Thinking About Me, 2nd Edition*. Think Social Publishing, Inc. San Jose, CA. www.socialthinking.com

Winner, M.G. (2007b). *Social Behavior Mapping*. San Jose, CA: Think Social Publishing, Inc. www.socialthinking.com

Wolfberg, P. (2003). *Peer Play and the Autism Spectrum. The Art of Guiding Children's Socialization and Imagination.* Kansas: Autism Asperger Publishing Company.

Zaks, Z. (2008). "Interventions for children with autism spectrum disorders: Major issues, major choices". *Autism Asperger's Digest,* January-February 2008. Arlington, TX: Future Horizons, Inc.

# About the Author

**Michelle Garcia Winner, MA, CCC** is a speech language pathologist who specializes in the treatment of individuals with social cognitive deficits: those with diagnoses such as Autism, Asperger Syndrome and Nonverbal Learning Disorder. In private practice in San Jose, California, she and her clinic staff work with individuals from 3 years old into adulthood who struggle with social thinking and related social skills.

The heart of her work is illuminating the often illusive and intangible world of social thinking, and developing practical strategies that can be easily used by parents, educators and service providers, across different environments, to teach social thinking and social skills. A pioneer and visionary in her field, her work is being applied not only to persons with autism and related disabilities but also more broadly to students in mainstream classrooms and to adults in vocational/professional settings in the U.S. and abroad.

Michelle is a prolific writer in the area of social thinking/social skills and travels internationally presenting numerous different workshops. She has been invited to train psychiatrists, psychologists, counselors, parents, educators and state policy makers on the importance of social thinking. Her goal is to raise awareness among administrators, educators and parents of the critical role social thinking and social skills play in every student's life, not just in achieving academic success, but for success in adulthood and life in general.

Michelle was awarded a Certificate of Special Congressional Recognition in 2008 for her pioneering work.

Michelle has two girls, Heidi and Robyn, who attend college and continue to keep her humble.

## Also by Michelle Garcia Winner

*Think Social! A Social Thinking Curriculum for School Aged Students*

*Inside Out! What Makes a Person with Social Cognitive Deficits Tick?*

*Thinking About YOU Thinking About ME, 2ⁿᵈ edition*

*Social Behavior Mapping:*
*Connecting Behavior, Emotions and Consequences Across the Day*

*Sticker Strategies to Encourage Social Thinking and Organizations*

*Superflex…A Superhero Social Thinking Curriculum*

*You are a Social Detective!*

*Worksheets for Teaching Social Thinking and Related Skills*

*Strategies for Organization: Preparing for Homework and the Real World*

*Social Thinking Across the Home and School Day*

*Social Thinking Posters for Home and the Classroom*